Love and a Lion

Toluwani King

WestBow Press books may be ordered through booksellers or by contacting:

WestBow Press
A Division of Thomas Nelson & Zondervan
1663 Liberty Drive
Bloomington, IN 47403
www.westbowpress.com
1 (866) 928-1240

ISBN: 978-1-5127-5645-6 (sc)
ISBN: 978-1-5127-5646-3 (hc)
ISBN: 978-1-5127-5644-9 (e)

Library of Congress Control Number: 2016915026

Print information available on the last page.

WestBow Press rev. date: 10/31/2016

Contents

What makes us King

My Love,

I write to you in the golden ambience of Sunday morning. Sat on the silver-brown couch set on a maroon patio of a Georgian house, I document brewed insight.

My horizon: towering trees and white-golden leaves; my horoscope: Love.

What I want to share with you is a function of thought and vision—what you must understand—makes me your pride.

Because you are, I shall tell a precise truth.

When father passed away, I took his name:

"Tortola Isaac Love"

Father had six children:

Tomato
I am
Pepper
Cranberry
Peach & Beans

To take a man's name is to take on their commission and inherit their fame. Father's commission was to love and cherish his family. In 'Abba Father's' name, Tori succeeded in carrying out his will—some would say—through me.

After giving his beautiful girls away—in holy matrimony, and his dear son had learned his way, I was relieved of father's commission, and settled into the responsibility of finding Myself: War! —For I had been so lost. And it didn't matter before—because I was under fathers thumb.

Now, I would set out to establish mine.

The residue of father's legacy lingered. What an air of majesty— to be handed such responsibility: the privilege of raising grown children; to inherit his friends, and his wealth; to intimate a satisfaction of wholeness when something so severe had been lost.

I thought it a Godly gift; an asset perhaps—the world would need. So I set out—arrogantly, to heal a world I thought was sick: my dire misgiving.

Quickly, I caught the world's cold, and submerged hollow. In an abyss of uncertainty, I found a new name: Hollow Sticks; I was the inside of a tall Bamboo stick. In time, I found there were many like me: Bamboo sticks, tall and beautiful on the outside and deeply tragic on the in.

Whatever it was I inherited from my father most certainly was not enough to heal these broken hearts. I needed more: more love; I needed more than my father; more God. And that's when I found Truelove.

King

Carrot Anna Tara Apple Tangerine Hope Tobi Love Deola Mark John Mohammed Love
Ireolu Abdulaziz Abba Paul Emmanuel Zainab Arab Rain King Batya Temmy Keisha
Anna Shola Mustapha Ike Kingsley Arinze Ese Baby April Marco Joseph Ibrahim
Zara Eshovo Abu Wafor Blessing Confidence Abubakar Aramide Valerie Dasha
Brijnath Dare Femi Kemi Mary Afor Abdulrazaq Julie Stephen Eguolo Kate Beatrix
Bukki Yetunde Emmanuel Rin-Rin Maryam Zuru Lukonde Augie Bamboosticks
James Ali Bee Olumide Phillips Charles Agutu Yosola Kuku Ife Peach Chisome
Abu Sugarcane Danny Deji Bolaji Lyfe Jennings Chichima Zara Inumidun
Honorable Onome AdenikeCharlotte Mayowa Charlie Simbi Yinka Tolu
Gayathri Muyiwa Deji Kunle Beans Foghor Bee Camil Junior Kelechi Ngozi
Funto Dupe Ugli Fruit Abadom Wild Blueberrie Igbo Red Apple Coconut
Pineapple Custard Apple Abo Chibueze Chinechezirim Yagazie Chinelo
God Ike White Chikezie Supreme Victoria Ajala Luck Ganiru Twins Idogbe
Good Ginikachukwu Andreea Olaniyi Hassana Ibekwe Agreement Wh
Hassan Iberedemobong Ifekristi Light Christ Igbo HereIbironke Family
Happiness Idaramfon Efik Ibibio Ife Mofoluwakemi Blessing Inn
Yoruba Cup Ire Madam Bomi Okpere Long Okwute Olabisi Oladele
Home Oladosu Moon Olajide Yejide Kno Olalekan Olaoluwajuwon
Lion Zaki Hausa Peter Hariya Zoputa Protector Uzodimma Gatee
Ayers Olaseni Easily Boysenberries Olayemi Timi Ifechi Ifede Love
Alive Hauwa Zauna Flowe Aduke Ifeoluwapo Ifetundun Love Sweet
Tree Igitioluwotilaiye Root Journey Ijeoma Lif Beef Ikechukwu Power
Pac Ikeoluwa Clementine Ikponmwosa Benin Leader Obi Heart
Igbo Emeka Obianauju Peace Zikorachukwud Paul Lewis Abu
Zoputan Sno Ileara Child Ilozumba Imbiana Unity Inegbedion
Oba King Good Character Nsedu Tiwa Kingship Kristibueze
Machie Sleepp ClementIretomiwa Blessing Kaodinakachi Destiny
Leaf Mojisola Fortune Obioma Gem Modupeore kayoed Mongo
Famous Nwamaka Patience Ndidi Maka Advantage Goodwill
Nkwo Market Creator Nwaoma Oban Obiefune Monjolaoluwa
Hausa Nagodeallah Nkeoma Good John Beauty Robert Chinwe
Uwailomwan Oluchi Chetachukwu Yetunde Olusola Utibe Marvelous
Okonkwo Ify Tope Mofe Felix Liah Pi Solomon Chinyere Paul Eber
BenjaminChiOlufemiOlugbala Olukayode Joy Olumoroti Stand
Olusegun Victory Yoruba Chinmakodim Udumelue Crown Honor
Pride Olorunyomi Olisa God Igbo Okechuku Destiny Isoken Conten
Itunu Iwenjiora Iyabo Iyawa Hausa Jaiyesimi Jesutise Jesus Jideofor
SpaRespect Juba Awakes Izukanne Light Ihekristi Christ Igbo Valerie
Carrisa Olatundun Sweet Kind Abaeze Watermelon Olive King Olato
Branch Igbo Guava Sharon Plum Orange Chimaobi Heart Sugarcane
Abayomi Water Coconut Abi Abu Yusuf Joy Yoruba Adaoma Lady
Yabanii Abayomrunkoje God Life Quince Raisins Durains Feijoa
Guava Clementine Maradol Sour Cactus Pear Saraki Barbados Charles
Cantaloupe Blood Orange Brown Turkey Fig Yemi Kemi Femi Monday
Sanitubi Yusuf Papaya Strawbery Abebi Hauwa Wale Prince Bay Itunu
Iyabo Page JJa Abegunde Jesus Abeni Abdurazaq Omotola Iya-beji Bowale
Sugarcane Chiemeka Chimezie Sugar Apple Naruto Abeo Cactus Peace
Tubosun Zainab Adewale Prince Anthony Chidubem Guave Abidemi Dew
Mango Otumba Kuku Sarut Abubakar Seun Tola Lola Prince Chilotam Kiki
Sasuke Abidugun War Rain Bankai Omotoriola Lola Adeniyi Tope Omotoso
Oluwa Ud Abiodun Naima Zakari Festival Love Peace Debra-Louise Adebambo
Crown Me Chimbuchim Kuku Abiodun Nike Ayelowo Brazil Abidemi Chigoziem
Cal Abdulahi Chikanma Efik Ibibio Ab Olumide Abioye Eleanor-Rose Adaora
Daughter Igbo Isamotu Olalekan Destitute Kokumo Jumoke Abioye Ibrahim
Abolanle Mohammed Strabery-Papaya Abomeli Achebe Goddess Precious Love
Gold Edel-Rose Haruna Achike Steady Winner Igbo Rami Achutebe Adebamgbe
Dwells Charles Absence Happiness Abiodun Zod Deola Carla Mojo Ajala Deniyi
Rose Anber JoyAda-afo Third Solabomi Yetunde Precious Yewande Paul Sukanmi
Olabisi Oyenikan Jospeh Adewale Rukewe Coco rIN-rIN Adamma Daughter Beauty
IgboAdankwo Oshoname Kiwi X Strawberry-Guava Adebisi Momo Adebiyi Batya Adebowale
Marian Adeboye Title Ajaka Top Segun Adedayo Tayo Adedeji Two-Iyabo Adedoyin Sweet
Tosin Adefolake Tobi Adejola Anna Igbo Red Apple Coconut Pineapple Custard Apple Abo
Chibueze Chinechezirim Yagazie Chinelo God Ike White Chikezie Supreme Victoria Ajala Luck
Ganiru Twins Idogbe Good Ginikachukwu Andreea Olaniyi Hassana Ibekwe

Summer 15'

Prelude

Sitting by the creek, a Lion strutted to me and asked,
"What's on your mind?"

I promised I'd write:

For Lion

"You are salt of the earth and God's kind breath."

The Apple Tree

1

Spirit and Youth

It started with an absolute truth:
"I am 'Love'."

For 'God' is love and
'Abba Father' is my Father.
Therefore, I am Love.

And where there was hate and a lie, I thought I would die.

I would learn there is life after death.

A life of power, and no regret, a
life of love— impassioned reward:

A love that will never die,
will never fail—
true love that lasts
always.

The Absurdity of Death

Dear Lion,

Once upon a time, there was a seed—hollow, and uniquely deep—beautiful and proud—strange, and full of mind.

Sown into the heavens, one day she blossomed into the moon.

Just like the moon, a cub grew—so did young 'Love' too.

Roar,
Love

Dear Edel—magnificent Queen,

I have known you in 'Spirit'. What a joy you have been. You truly are the emblem of dignity, and all that is complete and neat.

With all my heart, I bury you in God's precise love.

The soil is eternally fertile; it is God's spirit, God's truth, God's love, God's youth—God's life, wisdom and ubiquitous beauty. It is God's wealth, grace and never ending mercy.

As the sun sprouts to perpetual shine, may your good love never die.

May the countenance of our good-natured God shine upon you— as does the sun, this lovely earth.

Welcome to life, o beautiful Queen;
Welcome to joy, o hope of noble scene.

The strength of the heavens and my boisterous affection,

King

Life

So Love grew, and Love knew.

The forgetfulness of Hollow Sticks

All that once was, was now forgotten—but truth, faith, hope, and love.

And love...

The Apple Tree

The winters grew grayer each year. At its core, epicurean wanderlust: I dreamt of revelry amid a halting affair.

Without earthly father, I basked in the arms of the heavens and prayed me and mine well—for these lonely nights dulled my wild-orphaned heart.

"There must be more to life than a Victorian fire place and these scattered sheets night after night," I whispered, between dreams.

I longed to know my father. Perhaps, his love would set me free.

And so what was within was sought after, endearingly, on these lands, seas, and waters.

Dear Lion,

I can hear your giggle in the clouds—an all-too-welcome sound.

Let me lie at the depths of your cheek;

Cover me in the pit of your dimple, mild and moon.

And when the sun comes up, take me to the sands of your shores—where we like to dance.

Bless our souls as we dance on these still waters—quiet, and sincerely blue.

Bless our hearts as we dance.

Fill me up,
Love

Dear Father,

You are patient at every turn, Gentleman that You are. Shall I not be like You?

Here I am Lord.

Eagerly Yours,
Love

I advance, 'Abba Father' in my smile: what a love affair—what tender design.

...

Having seen a world that truly was my oyster, full of love and eager smiles, I crossed Winton's wintry boarders into Matakar's golden sun where I settled in her reflection, Homeland. An audacious site she was.

With my lewd mind heedfully occupied, I blazed an unstoppable trail, leaving value behind—along with it, broken hearts.

But where there was fleeting lust and dying affection, 'Love' remained. It was in this love I loved a boy.

About a boy

Mother and Father had passed away. In their absence, we remained: Love, a brother and four exquisite sisters. What wouldn't we do for one another? We forged a bond stronger than brotherhood. We were united in our love and absolute care. How we thrived in that care!

Recurrently, I attended Bean's Parent-Teacher Association (PTA) meetings.

When appearing, I would take quiet pleasures in being the youngest parent there. Mothers who were not puzzled by my presence were simply baffled and in inquiring awe of my composure. I paid it no mind; I was there for my brother, my burgeoning child.

Dear Lion,

Sometimes I want to live a childhood I left behind.

Forced to be parent at seventeen—a privilege I am most grateful for—I dance in a childlike state I fear may never cease.

How I love life's great thrills.

Love,
Love

In a long wind at one of these quite entertaining sessions, I took a stroll down Evergreen's cloisters, and saw a boy.

He seemed a sad, beautiful boy. His shoulders were keen; his posture humble, and his big-litte eyes said much more than I fathomed a child could.

He was thirteen and by himself.

I asked, "Are you lost, child?"

I forget what he said. But I knew he was my kin.

From that day, Mother left two magnificent boys and four angelic girls in my care.

Fraternity

Over the years, the boys loved my visits. I would come with edible treats, and what they called 'eye candy' in the form of a lawyer friend or chef friend; a local charmer, full of life and good spirit, eager to teach.

Zealous to see them do well, they would sit with my boys and share their success stories, as intended. Each tale ended with an admirable moral lesson the boys will soon forget. How they taught anyway.

I spoke about Beans and Cocopine all the time, and everyone that loved me knew I loved them. And they loved them too.

About a Mother

Love grew between my boys and me, and in time, garnered inquiry. Cocopine's mother had now learned a strange man had fed her little boy life, good nature, and true affection. And so we met at another one of these quite entertaining events.

We quickly learned we had a lot in common. I gained a fondness for Cocopine's mother, and over time, learned about her wars, sorrows, and dreams.

Carrot grew up in the mountains far south of here in what I imagine was a very large compound, full of trees and dancing machines. She was gentle, kind, and a dreamer—until her first union.

Little girls dream, and if daughter was anything like her mother, Carrot dreamt of a castle. In it was a love that was patient, kind, and did not suffer.

Against all odds, life was life; love—love, and commitment, war.

Her marriage came and in time, took its toll.

Dear Lion,

I wonder, "Is it just you I'm writing to?"

I struggle to recall.

Perhaps I don't remember things all too well because I want to forget.

If that were true, I am forced to ask why. For if it were the fear of reliving a pain, I fear not—I have known deep sorrow.

What is it then? A lack of fondness for the past? A vehement desire to survive?

If I am Love, must I not forgive, must I not forget?

What is the point of intermittent regret?

Is this a story that must be read or a thought that must be heard?

To personify a country, I would say Homeland was narcissistic—and her people sharing in the same characteristics.

For if love is patient, kind, and all of the virtues in the Bible's 1 Corinthians 13, then none of us is Love, or in love—just an exasperation of aspiration, a relentless drive that insists on its own way.

Carrot was expelled from her matrimonial home after a decade. Her husband, the man of her dreams, wanted children. Carrot did not bear, and he could not bear it.

A narcissistic Samaritan—a function of Carrots perception—learned of Carrot's beauty and plight and quickly took delight. He promised to love her. I don't know what promises she made, but Carrot told me that he failed.

Then one of Homeland's wealthiest men, Chief Taincy planted his seed in Carrot and in nine months a light was born. Many years later, I would call her Lemon.

Over the years, Chief Taincy gave my dear friend—and she had become truly dear—two more gorgeous children: a girl who would be a nation's treasure and friend, and a prince who became his dream.

Chief Taincy grew weary of this love affair—like the others he had—and in insisting on his way, threw them out.

Her heart now with fright, and children who by now had learned Cathedral floors from these nights without shelter—without drawers, had learned prematurely, "a harshness of life".

Hearts—one-by-one were replaced with stone; little pieces of sand turned into rock and eventually, unyielding ore.

But how could I have known?

Was I there?
When did I ever see past faith and hope?

For love is love, and God, God. And all I knew was love. And all I knew was God.

I was keen to help this woman; I was desperate to try. I do not recall waiting for good graces to guide or God's decent advice to provide.

I was matter, and took His nature into my hands.

...

The declination of Love

With his mother's blessing, Cocopine had started spending his holidays with me, and "little Love", Beans. We were three brothers— by resolve, in love. I took them everywhere—we lived; we adored.

The tides tore through the shores, and we were one.

As a responsible father would, I started to plan the boys' prospects. I wanted only the best for them. I was going to sell everything if I had to.

We inherited a trust fund after mother and father departed. Therefore, Beans had the freedom to attend school anywhere he pleased. Cocopine however, did not inherit such luxury from pain. So I set out to create a trust in his name—that he may be accorded the same wealth good graces gave.

In time, fate was kind.

I sought balance in our merriment; I loved both boys fairly and dearly.

On some nights, we would drive over to Carrot's so that Cocopine spent quality time with his mother. After a tuck-in, Carrot and I would stay up till the middle of the moon, talking.

We gabbed about everything; she became my best friend.

I learned her passions and reverie. She was strong and determined—especially now, to fight to the end; as if for the first time, she had learned to love herself.

I was inspired by her affection.

The boys were fourteen. They had three more years in High school before further edification.

My best friend wanted to build a coterie that administered a clever method of developing children in an evolving country. I was excited, and quite frantic to help. "This was her time!" I soliloquized—"It was time for Carrot to finally get what she wanted and not the potent cards it appeared life had dealt."

"Could we be partners? Is it possible that we could build something beautiful; something that added value?" I conceived. But more than value, and serving country, "could I help to give her power? The power to send her little boy to the best schools—as a function of her hard work, and genuine genius"—what I thought perhaps was every mothers dream. And I sought to help make all of her dreams come true—in every respect of a woman's dream: Carrot's dream.

In retrospect, I surmise: Who was I?
Was I God—maker of dreams and true love!
If I am His son, what is my position?
And what part must I play?

Did my alacrity cause my dismay?

When is a God-complex developed?
When does resolve become a God-complex?
And when is a good intention simply good?

The thought of using Cocopine's Education fund to fuel Carrots' dreams was born: "I bet if well-managed, Carrot will kill two birds: build a profitable enterprise and from it, secure the resources to send our excellent boy to the best schools".

I never intended to stay. My interests were far away.

We had time: three years. There was a structure. There was a plan.

A Happy Family

Dear Lion,

This is a somber story.
And it has made me terribly sad.

Roar,
Love

"Have you ever seen trees from the clouds?" I think them tall-dots.

From the highest heights, I saw seven dots: six siblings, my children—one mother, my best friend.

Like leftover corn on a cob, we were the only ones: Love's gift to each other—or so I thought, the romantic I thought I was.

One Saturday morning, I set out with Cocopine and Beans—on a date at the silver screen.

As always, choice made it an amusing thing.

When we returned, we met a young lady in the living room. She was gold-skinned. I could tell she was intelligent—her composure made it so. She stood to greet me, and I answered fairly.

In a trice of polite banter, I learned she was Cocopine's sister.

She was immediately someone I took interest in. She was brilliant, and appeared to have a gentle soul. She had just returned from University for the holidays. She was a calm talker, and appeared wise beyond her years.

She took Cocopine home that night, after she was warmly welcomed into my sites.

Now, we were eight; Mother left me five resplendent girls, two brave boys, and a refined best friend—to love and adore.

I was twenty-five.

Golden Retriever

She was nineteen, a heroine councilor and dear confidant. We exchanged emails when she was in university. I admired her strength, courage and wisdom. She surmounted favorite sister and charming friend. Soon, she met my girls. Well received, she quickly became cherished; she was ours, as we were hers.

In her, I saw stallion—a true champion. In her, I saw possibility, prospect and progress. I took avid interest in her comfort and keep; I would see to it she got what she needed, as I did her little brother, Cocopine and sister, Strawberry.

Now mothers were seven sweet girls, and two rather happy boys.

I loved them all.

Inspired by her, I mused ways to grow the family business and strengthen her name—"what a mélange of talent!"—quietly, I deliberated.

My heart brimmed with joy as I thought cleverly on ways to serve our country as a family.

She offered judicious advice to that avail, and progressively we prevailed.

A Lapse in Judgment

After their decease, I lost my glee for birthday parties. With indifference emerged a dive in appetite for many other vanities.

Over the years, friends and acquaintances would arrange surprise birthday parties. Never surprised, I would sneak out of soiree to a quieter place, to celebrate 'Truelove'—whose grace had made living a great deal so far.

Twenty-six, was no different. I snuck out with a box of cupcakes, and made my way to Carrot's place.

We celebrated as a family.

Carrot's first daughter saw me off that night. Sat on the bonnet of my car, she held me tight for my goodbye. She wrapped her skinny body around me, and placed the tip of her thumb on the base of my head—fondling my occipital nodes, as she wrapped the rest of her right hand fingers around my neck. It was the warmest hug I ever felt.

I feared her affection, and so I abstained.

My heart was not hers, nor was it mine or anyone else's—it was Love's—Truelove's.

Dear Edel,

Could the heavens smell better than your hair?

Blossom of grace, bloom and grow;
Strengthen my home,

Restore my soul.

Love always,
Papa

As bonds grew stronger, ambitions grew wilder. One day, sitting in Carrot's living room, I suggested we use Cocopine's education fund as capital to fuel Carrot's dreams. Carrot was terribly pleased with the idea—I was elated too.

I loved this woman. And I knew—if given the chance, the stars wouldn't stop her shine.

She asked how our business partnership would work. I asked her to indicate her preference. She replied, "equal stakes". We entered agreement to secure Cocopine's fate. The conditions set were safe:

> I will share my interests in company equally with her daughter. In return, she will act as financial controller, and support her mother's administration.

The second:

> Whatever revenue her daughter and I received will go into Cocopine's education fund for as long as he chose to remain in school.

We all agreed.

All was well in my kingdom; dreams were coming true. With everyone well taken care of, "I'll be off soon".

Love and Education

They grow up so fast—little boys. Soon they become young men; cast off naivety, and care very little for childish things.

My brothers had become strong—poised in love, and an abundance of God's word. We had created a trust "Truelove" adored—and we were not the only ones.

Carrot's daughter and I had built a diamond rapport. The seed of romance sprouted into roots beneath our friendship. I could not act: she was in university, and I was dreaming of revelry.

I had great love and respect for my brother's sister— Carrots daughter—and knew the consequence of knowing her skin:

My heart knew one heart, and commitment to another soul was far farfetched. I was loyal to my perception of love: a one-sided fondness for people; a tenderness that could heal a broken wing— with kindness and a kiss; adulation that made dreams come true. I feared being loved by a single soul—rosily, would take that love away from me. I feared a woman that needed more than my perceived ability to give—as proof of my commitment to never leave; I feared a shallow heart. I really did.

I never knew mine was what I feared so deep.

A Lovers dream

I dreamt I'd fall in love with the most beautiful woman in the world. I thought I had an eye for these things—and so, wanted a beauty that was special, divine and mine. She had a good heart, and cherished people. She loved me, and my love—was faithful to God, and His Word. Who was a physical manifestation of the grace and wisdom of the Holy Spirit—strong and comforter, meek and brilliantly wild—elegantly sensible; nurturer, and giver of life.

We would know our inheritance and so would be affably bold. The world would be our oyster, so we would never be anxious; never grow old. We would be sound-minded, full of love and God's immaculate word. We would travel all over the world to see our lands and break bread with their Lords—all God's children. And wherever we went, we would be light unto that world—as 'Truelove' intends.

We will elevate to heights many will see, and shine brightest—so all will acknowledge our Father is King—who is Truelove indeed.

"O Queen of Queens,

Ruler of Earth; fit for a mighty
and humble Prince; a son of man,
a servant of God.

I seek you in my heart and Spirit
secretly.

Where the world is full of lies
and poison, you are a precious
diamond worth protecting. Reveal
to me, the heavens where you
lay—that I may lay with you, in
God's grace.

I pray for increase.
Bless me with faith."

Hollow Sticks

The softness of her friendship reminded me of that dream. A dream I
dreamt when I was only seventeen. Before the world, and its choppy
grind—its arrogant heart, and odd aching sounds.

She was sensible and kind, deeply patient and eager to be mine. She
was good with God, and a rebel to the world. She appeared wise and
sensible, and I enjoyed her company remarkably.

Her feelings for me were well-known and mine, a gasp for certainty.

To indulge will be doom—a heart like mine will destroy if not smashed into. I dreamt of a passion as deep and as wild as the oceans—an explosion that will kill me, annihilate her, and let love be—our dead bodies, the perfect soil for "Truelove" to breed.

I was still unavailable, and so I stowed. Dreading the thought of doing right by her, I insisted I could not date a student: my mind and body were terribly spontaneous, and my wanderlust will leave her wondering, lost—what I couldn't bear for my deep appreciation for education.

She understood—but insisted she will wait. I believed her. At the same time I hoped she wouldn't; I hoped that in the three years to graduation, a practical man—with sensible reasoning would sweep her off her feet, and carry her away to a righteous place.

I was a dreamer, and was very much alive—"a rare and complicated beauty," Orange said, "not for the fainthearted but for the brave".

She was my sister, and like other kin, I wished hers would be a very simple thing.

My fair friend wouldn't stir. She insisted on my heart, as she waited patiently to embark.

When apart, I romanticized the ideal of us—King and Queen—ruling admirably in humble submission to the Heavens and our dreams. I thought about her qualities, or what I perceived them to be:

She was *graceful*
Intelligent
Godly
Appeared *prudent*
She was *wise*
She *understood* and *appreciated* my *dreams,* as I did hers.

And they were all coming true.
With budding ambitions, I thought I needed help.

And soon began to believe notion would help relieve my stress.

"'Mama and Papa', 'Truelove's' perfect blend"
Beans

My Helper

I needed help to raise my Boys.
I needed to create the kind of
wealth that helped to secure their
curiosities; these young men had
bigger dreams than me.

I needed help to grow God's
Kingdom on earth—to spread a
wild consuming fire that lit the
heart of man with tender flames
that never went away.

I needed help to make good dreams come true.

I needed help to live—for I
suffered spells of deep grief.

I needed help to remember, and
not forget that "I am";

I never needed until now.

With good purpose and resolve
to love, I needed help with the
magnitude of my commission,
my true love.

It was my perception of need that created a notion, a seed; a first
disciple, like me—my very own 'Mrs. Me'.

The great stall before the next chapter

Dear Lion,

How I dread this part.
For my heart does not write if it is not right.

Love

Me and Mrs. Me

If ever I did marry, I fancied the sentiment of marring family. A comprehension inspired by a need for absolute trust and loyalty—built on a premise: family never fails.

I never quite asked these questions:

What is family?
What does it mean to have family?
Who is my family?

I thought these questions were for pessimists. I was Love—full of hope and faith. And all of what was love, and had love in them, were my family.

"I had a big family!"—with budding ambitions to expand, I loved all fiercely!

I saw 'her' essence and perhaps all I wanted to see. Our relationship started at the depths of our dreams.

I loved her from the inside, and pushed through to the surface of her skin.

She was family. My love for her was simple: unselfish. Not as fiery or deeply passionate as other love affairs but patient, kind and submissive. I admired it: the gentleness of my affection. I admired what I thought to be her loyalties, enduringness and selfless devotion.

I wondered, "is this God's love; is this 'Truelove'?"

Graduation came.

I saw her. Not her essence, or devotion. I saw a tower of pure golden, glorious skin. She was divinely formed—in a tight, beautifully sewn black dress. She was taller than every woman in the crowd, and only had eyes for me.

For the first time, I was infatuated. I wondered why I hadn't seen her in this light. Too busy loving a sibling to see a woman. Too diligent caring for a child to acknowledge a Queen—and what a queen she appeared to be—a Queen who would rule over queens, my Queen.

Pure and golden, I hesitated before I committed.
Eventually, I submitted.
We advanced, hand-in-hand—heart-in-heart.

Dear Lion,

I cherish you.

Love

The Birth of Cruelty

We grew up in a love-hut—my sisters and me. The very fabric of our existence was my mother's touch. My father was wise, intelligent and a great teacher. We grew up in love—in a little garden, made just for us.

We were taught good character and forgiveness, good graces, and persistence. We were taught how to love.

Father worked with the government during the day. And at night, he taught about the constellation and stars. During the holidays he took us on interstate drives, while he taught about the savannas and sands. His was deeply charismatic and a gem of pure intelligence.

Mother was gentle and kind. She had a smile that lit the darkest dungeons, and hushed the harshest dragons. Mother was 'Truelove', and her name was beautiful.

Both English literature enthusiasts, they taught finer diction and excellent etiquette. In doing so, father made us read to him every night. He would yell "louder!" gleefully, as we stammered through Georgian text in front of his office desk—just before bed.

"I didn't know hatred until I knew love."

Time to go to Bed

It was nearly time for school. My boys were bright, and over the moon. Eager to tell their tales, they lay in summer's slight hay—waiting, as time raced to their resumption dates.

Meanwhile, Carrot had built a successful business and good school. What wholesome pleasure to see her joy. Carrot was well, and in good form. She had come into her own, and sat on a comfortable throne.

It wasn't only Carrot doing well, her daughter and I were merry, and on our way—securing erupting heights and roaming breathtaking sites.

She was fair, and certainly my-girl.

Trilled to send my boys off, I urged Carrot to pay.

Delinquent Love

In a mother-daughter contention on the matter of fees, Carrot advised cavalierly she could not keep her end of the deal. My fair lady affirmed she knew it would be so—as if it were a thing well known.

I was lost and confused. Twisted, I felt used. I wondered why she let me enter deal if she was sure of her mothers ill.

Was I overthinking this?

Perhaps she hoped things had changed and her mother progressed unblemished matriculate.

In wonder, I began to feel unsafe.

> *More than me was a boy that needed to be.*
>
> *So I dust off my hurt, and folded my sleeves, and prayed these gold mines were eager to please.*
>
> *Off to school! Cocopine's time was due.*
>
> *I prayed fervently he'd be there soon.*

...

An E in English altered pace,
and kept Cocopine's prep school far
away.

Next year we hope we get an A; that ought to keep these
butterflies away.

Cocopine was not going to school anymore. He would have to wait another year to re-write his English paper. Deeply sad, we spent the next few days in wallowed embrace.

"Cocopine bitter because he was seventeen and
eager to start a football career in Winton."
"Love sad because he did not understand."

Greater Heights

Dear Lion,

Once upon eternity was the truth. It was all there was—the only thing beautiful enough to be, or write about.

The truth is the morning; the skies above, and the evenings; the stars in the night. The truth is love; what makes us feel alive—Lion of this champion tribe.

The truth is your smile: strength of the heavens and these proud lands.

The truth is God's love—an infinite reward.

Love always,
Truelove

In the depth of self-pity, and what now appeared to be Carrot's blatant disregard for Cocopine's fees, I released my consciousness into higher peaks. With guarded heart, I hoped for better sight.

I saw.

And that's when it started.

Lofty Sight

I started to wonder, "What truly was the nature of my relationship with Carrot's daughter?" Thrown off by her utter indifference and lack of care for what I loved, my first doubt was born.

Dear Lion,

What does it mean to love?
How do I show it—How do you know it?

Is it the strolls we take or the hearts we break?
Is it in our talks or the way we walk?

Is "I love you" enough?

Love is the treasure in the fold, the gift that never grows old.

Love is loving the things that I love—nature; the birds and their
songs;

Love is everything I see.
Love is loving you, truly.

Yours,
Truelove

Getting to know her better, I had learned a few things:

She had a squabble with her mother that never ended—as do all
mothers, with the first of their little girls perhaps. Drawn to its gist, I
would play matchmaker March and May.

They will settle their quarrels only to part again.

I was her escape, her quiet place. Curious about her agenda, I gave her all my space.

Quite alike, her Father came; her love for him was very much the same: she indulged him were there was gain, and parted ways, much to his dismay.

A thousand red flags flew—what I saw at first it seemed was not true.

In my-love, I saw pretense and what was easy became choleric stress.

This love that once grew, soon became a lustful avenue.

An Abyss of Broken Stars

We had started talking about a future together. I was devoted to our cause, or my perception of what it was. Diligent to my love, I announced our engagement as we discussed. Though unsure—I thought, "God will use this deeply baffling affair as testimony to exalt His name".

Even though saddled and ready for my gallop of faith, I stopped believing my-love was grail. I feared what I perceived was her intention but I wasn't sure. It didn't matter I thought, "in Love, ill intensions fall"—for love simply conquers all.

What a credulous being I was.

At the same time, a hideous curiosity that would destroy us was born.

By now, obsessions of her assumed intension occupied my thoughts. In my eyes, she became bitter and sweet, and in time, I couldn't tell which was which.

So, I called her Lemon.

Lemon

Lemon was always five feet and inches tall. She was always young; she was always old: "A cocktail of paradoxes" I suppose. In knowing her, I became amused by the depth of her intellect and what also appeared to be a pit of emptiness.

Lemon grew up on an Apple tree. Afraid of heights, she feared the sites. Clinging on for life, she held on tight.

Finding comfort in her discomfort, Lemon watched the day and night. She envied life, as it unraveled below her: little apples emerged big Apples, green apples quirked greener, and eventually, bloomed red.

And on the grass beneath the tree, she admired the little girls who read and the tenderfoot boys who played in the sand.

Lemon read their stories in the books that were sent up into the tree. She liked to live vicariously through their songs, and only dreamt of true love.

With no shelter atop the tree, the nights were cold, and the winds a horrid reality. Lemon cried in the storms and in the chaos of life on top a tree. When the Apples bickered, she grappled for her existence. Learning necessary means, she prevailed.

Autumn came, and winters fell. All of what was the Apple tree withered but Lemon dwelled—rock, and a hard place, her heart won't break. She had learned the winter, and had become its pain.

Winter

Winter is sweetest when it is not cold, and does not break your bones.
Winter is romantic under warm clothes and
emollient cracklings of fire.

Winter however, takes its toll.

Lemon—now young and beautiful, took after winter.
But Apple trees bloom in the spring. In a land of Apples and Easter,
Lemon feared her winter, and hid its sting. Graceful and poised deep,
wherever she fell, her snowflakes sparkled—bright and bleak.

The curse of a Black Diamond's White Light

Lemon's light sparkled through the depths of the city—turning heads and Apples.

She had an odd perfection; what I thought was a beautiful darkness, and in her eyes, doubt painted a sparkly void.

So I bought a ring to perpetuate ardent sight. At its core, a big black rock—deep and pure—around focus, petite dark diamonds encased in brilliant white rhombi.

The ring, what I thought was a savvy metaphor for Lemon's wintery sparkle and deep black cold, now sat on her finger—with a prayer: "that one day 'that deep elegant black' will turn into a complete heavenly white".

I prayed it silently, hopefully, faithfully.

Lemon loved her ring. She ogled night and day. To her, it was the most beautiful thing she had ever seen. And it was.

We did not however, share the same interpretation.
She was happy—I was hopeful.

Love in Winter

The town criers carried the news of our engagement, and the local gossips set to inquire. News will soon reach my sisters about Carrot and some awful old tales. My sisters would also learn of mine and Carrots collapsed concern—despite eager attempts to keep it veiled. They were anxious, and did not hide their mind.

After several failed attempts to wean me off her, they broke away hoping perhaps in isolation I wouldn't stay.

My boys' cold feet followed. In the chaos of it all, I prevailed, oblivious to forsake.

I didn't understand it—How could a person be
so uncharitably despised!

I was upset and deeply sad: "I was intrigued!"
How could everyone just leave!

Were we not loved? Were we not taught to Love!
"Our mother was Love", I exclaimed—when
I pleaded with the girls to stay.

Who are we to judge!
Who was I to judge?

They had judged her, and so had I. And now, she was condemned—without reprieve.

I understood how one could react to the tales. But exile—I thought, was a tad too lame. "I will not leave her!" so I chose to stay.

Not only out of compassion or what I believed was love. But I had a concern that felt like a call. I thought Lemon was special and her heart was pure. Albeit perceived abyss and shortness of stead, I thought there was something peculiar—ardent instead:

"A golden flower too shy for the sun. A rose not for the spring or just anyone; a peculiar blossom," that's what I saw.

There was something in Lemon deeper than my perception, more powerful than their intuition—something worth protecting—worth dying for.

I believed it earnestly.

I would protect and love her—even if it cost me everything.

It did.

These Harsh Times

What now appeared to be rumors of Carrot's past didn't help matters.

When I was impatient and caught-up in my sorrows, my affair with kind Carrot narrowed—and at its depths, I appreciated Lemon's breath even less.

In patience and love however, Carrot was simply a survivor; a brilliant one at that—what I thought was deceitful perhaps—superb, nonetheless. Always thinking value, I wondered how well her talents could be put to greater use.

I wished also that she wouldn't put what others believed was her selfishness and improvised need to survive before our friendship. I cherished it completely.

She was deeply influential and intellectually seductive when I wasn't apprehensive. I thought she would make a fine leader under better circumstances.

I thought I knew her. I thought I loved her.

While I appreciated her productive talents, the world I lived in would make no effort to agree. Frightening rumors—it seemed had concealed her better deeds.

I would learn later she wouldn't mind.

And that's what I liked about her—she was bold in seeming plight.

There was now one soul in my care.
I had abandoned my post and my children.

Lemon had inherited the sins of her mother and was tried as well.

The other fruits thought she was a pretender, with an agenda. I argued she was deeply misunderstood, and urged them to be good. I thought I knew better. I contended anyway—a soft plea to urge them to stay. How I wanted Lemon to be loved.

The other fruits—I feared—had now seen what I saw, and felt sorry for. Where they were livid, I was worried; nervous I was the same, and not even my family knew my name.

Still, they did not understand my attraction, and urged me to refrain.

She knew hate, and fear— all too well. I thought I knew what she needed; I thought I could help. I thought she needed to be taught to love herself. I thought she needed to be taught to care.

> Who would teach her love when she did not trust our affair—
> when mine treated her with hate and distasteful disdain?
> Who would teach her love when she was afraid?
>
> Who would care for her thoughtfully?
> Who would instruct her benevolently?

I thought and prayed: "A good father would stay".

The Tree of Life

I sought Lemon's father; he blessed me and gave me her hand.

He saw what I saw in her, and was quite impartial about his take. He knew I loved her, he knew I'd obey.

In spite of the harrowing stories I heard from Carrot and Lemon, I respected him. I admired his intellect, and fine judgment.

Chief Taincy was truly wise and an angel in disguise. He was stylishly handsome and a renowned writer in the local community. He lived in a big white house in the Orange County.

Many loved and revered the good Chief, and in the Apple state—he was a leader and not afraid.

Occasionally, I would drive over to the OC for his council on heart and social matters.

During one of our chitchats, I shared candid reflections on Lemon, and what appeared to be our fix. He listened and sympathized utterly.

Lemon had started work. The commute from Carrot's was tough and our tradition would not let her live with me until we were legally married.

Chief Taincy offered a fair solution to what appeared to be our quandary.

The Celery's

Dear Lion,

How to describe Royalty; Majesty; Strength and Honor;

Divine conquests, answered prayers, a shout of worship—praise!

The old monarchs used castles for emblems and Countesses sought crowns. The gods sought beauty and the Vikings conquered lands.

My thoughts are of a triumphant King.

'Roar'

The Celery's were an echo from heaven—our answered prayers:
A prayer from a father who wanted to do right by his daughter—for
all the wrong she heard he had done; a prayer from a man who knew
his friend needed a father more than a lover.

Chief Taincy knew his daughter; from what she told me, I thought he
was co-author of her suffering. He would do right by her. Through
the Celery's, he will do for her that which he was unable to for many
years. Faith had offered redemption—with it, his solemn vow to
succor.

"The Celery's will give her good love that will fill her up and condition
her heart to receive the love of a man—who was not 'her father'; who
was not 'unkind'. Their love would teach her to love a world that was
'her father'; that was 'unkind'."

"'Their love' will usher in a grace that will capture her heart, and
break it."

Chief Taincy—for my sake—would call upon his old mate, and ask a
favor I won't forget.

Lemon was soon in a comfortable home on Celery Drive—a few minutes walk from mine—living with a man she now called "Daddy". Daddy was a good man, and he took good care of Lemon. Daddy had a wife Lem called "Mummy". Mummy called her child. They lived and loved happily.

Separate from what she knew, Lemon had finally found a home—a place unlike a chilly tree; a safe place she could be, and thrive happily.

"She will be loved here", raised and fed "good"; she will learn to be kind, pleasant, and will not be misunderstood. She had not experienced such finality in stability.

She would be taught the love of a grounded father and the faith and loyalty of a fair mother.

And I did my best to show her the love of man. I failed several times—I made her happy, I made her sad.

I prayed the balance of a father and mother's love will erect a sturdy grace to forgive. I prayed that prayer for a while—and little by little, Lemon's yellow gyred gold.

.

Moments to matrimony, Lemon got in a tiff with an Aunty Apple from my category. Aunty Apple was summoned by Lemon's new mother, Mummy. Mummy did not like how upset Lem was when she found her that morning.

Aunty Apple arrived at the Celery's on a casual Sunday morning. Whatever was shared was not heard. I learned later it was a few odd stories of Carrot that made Mummy worry.

Lemon loved Carrot, and did not like Aunty Apple's very blunt tone when they had discussed her mother that morning.

Mummy handled the matter maturely, and soon, closed that story.

But fairytales don't always last, and soon the world would drop its mast.

The Celery's would have to go—and sweet Lemon would be left alone.

Newborn love was soon misplaced and lacked somewhat in first place.

Lemon was devastated and truly bitter. I was conquered and terribly sad—I had never seen Lemon so bewildered.

She loved the Celery's and I was sure they loved her too.

Now without father, my bittersweet fruit was left under the moon.

She will go back home—where she will unlearn all of what she had cultivated; "all of what made her gold," or I will create a safe place for her to continue to grow.

I wanted her close, safe and in my care. In a place I hoped the world wouldn't sneer:

A place I would strive to finish what the good Shepard's started— thinking task more important than a need to be loved, or a care for our love.

The Lemon Tree

2

The Lemon Tree

I quite fancied the thought of legalizing my rapport with Cocopine. By marring his sister, he would be my brother-in-heart, and law. I hoped merging our families would secure a deeper comfort in what had now become his home—and Lemon would finally have her own.

Even though we didn't see anymore, I kept his room in good order, and hoped for a time we all would gather. I cherished the notion of celebration—a time we all forgave; a time we eradicated strange. But that notion—it seemed—had become nothing but a dream. Lemon and I were carving our own path now. I left what I knew and had built, to cleave onto her youth.

Lemon was my success story, my attempt at reticent glory— that genuine prize that aligns the stars. I ignored all the flags, and looked up to our risen mast—what was now our life.

Though shattered by my loss, I was spellbound by who I was: I was a man of my word. I made Lemon a promise, and sought guidance when I feared I wouldn't keep it.

Our marriage Counselors were wise and guided spirits. Over the course of our Christian interaction, they learned the content of our hearts and the depth of allied intention.

After faithfully attending several sessions, they insisted we wait. We heed, but eventually disobeyed.

Eager to pass the tests, we plotted a course that offered less stress.

She wanted to be with me, in our home. I wanted a place for her to grow.

I announced the prospects of a court wedding to my sisters, after I pursued Chief Taincy and Carrots' blessings. They asked me kindly to wait.

Stubborn and insisting on our way, we decided on a court date.

*Do you want to learn a lesson, or do you want
to hearken your hearts and listen?*

"Young fruits, always in a hurry. Perhaps someday
we will learn to listen to 'Mummy'".

Elope

It was a simple affair. We looked darling and a power couple—
everyone stared.
For witnesses, we invited a cousin from her side and an old friend
from mine.

Lemon was thrilled; she finally had her own.
I was pleased; Lemon had a safe place to grow.

Disparity: A finite Consciousness

Tick-Tock Tick-Tock Tick-Tock

Time. Time is an apparent object in regret. How it passes in comfort and no stress. There is no time in love. Love is like the wind—flows from nowhere and goes nowhere.

When I was, I had nowhere to go. Now, these walls are defined and time is on my mind.

In the center of our living, I realized I had never noticed time—not until now.

Undeterred by perennial warning, I had delivered on ambition: Lemon was in my home.

In the first few days of promise, she was my Siberian wallflower, and I was her Monarch butterfly. I fluttered for her nectar, and she gave me her heart.

And when she had consumed my wings, we lay in the center of our living—watching the big clock that hung loosely from the ceiling.

What to do now...

I wondered.

Right! Finish task: 'Be a good dad!'

But she was my wife. Why was I so eager to complete task?
And besides,

How much Father could I be?
How much Pa could I give?
How much God did I truly have in me?

I had now chosen to share my consciousness with Lemon. Praying that it was good and I was enough to fill her up. I gave her my smile, laugh, joy and style. I gave her my wealth and all my love.

She gave her courage and submission. She gave her love.

She gave what she could give, when I asked—and when she took, she took, and she tried. She tried desperately to give me what she did not have. And I gave and I gave—a thing perhaps, she did not need—hoping desperately to believe.

How foolish of me: to give a thing that could not be received. To need a thing that could not be given.

Now off the moon—and avidly soon, I realized I was alone in my room. My family and loved ones had forsaken me. Lemon felt greatly reviled, and the reason for this frenzied season. She became angry and full of hate. She despised our love and the life I gave. Ours became a truly sour fate.

I urged her to swallow her pride and make merry with our sides. For how could we love in so much hate?

My-love now scorned won't change—her mind became vague. She made my plea quite the debate.

Lemons lips now full of bitter wits, made it harder to kiss.

No matter what I tried, Lemon chose her citrus over my sweet side. And so, our-love began to die.

Tick-Tock Tick-Tock Tick-Tock

Ashes

Chief Taincy had now learned we were living together and so he came to visit.

I was rapt—I desired his approval. Lemon on the other hand was apprehensive: "sour wounds from history's hooks".

Still, Chief Taincy tried to make things right, and I urged Lemon to be kind.

We welcomed him with open arms and fine wine. He looked at me and thought me a brave man—he did not think I would go ahead after everyone ran scared.

He had heard the stories, and the mystical worries—"How 'Aunty Kiwi' prayed, and saw in a vision: 'our love will fade'" or "how he and Carrot were the Devil and orchestrator of our acerbic fate". He showed us compassion.

He seemed a simple man. He thought I meant well. He wanted us to do well.

That night, he left in good cheer but not without advice—this time, the last I would let myself hear, for the sake of my dying affair. He said, "Beware. If not catered for, gold looses its shine, and silver shops unlocked, make an arena for raging-bulls".

I had no idea what he meant.

It didn't matter to me. I had made my choice. I would bear my cross.

So he said goodbye, and I saw him off.

The next few months living together were a mentally agonizing toil. But it didn't matter—I had learned most marriages were:

"I complained about everything, and she didn't seem to care".

I felt like a Landlord who had just taken in a demanding guest. I would present better ways to do things, and she would protest she didn't need my help. In retrospect, I conceive we were trying to do our best.

My efforts were not appreciated—her efforts, the same.

We started to lose admiration for one another, and slowly began to change.

She needed me to not have such high tastes. I wanted her to open her mind, and stretch her faith.

Her deep insecurities made teaching anything a catastrophe to learn:

- Feedback was damaging criticism.
- To suggest a better way—however polite, meant she was barbaric and not right.

She was impossible to talk to or reason with. Provoked in time, I became stubborn, and tyrant in my teaching, and soon, a bore to employ.

Our reality excited cruelty. And when we were cruel, we broke for better and worse:

Better, because when we broke, an old and perhaps destructive-self died, giving way for something new, or at least the prospect of paradise.

Worse, because when we broke Lemon's heart hardened toward me—making iniquity harder to forgive.

Our relationship was not what she expected: It made her tart; "I was sent to save her!"—it made her mad, it was so sad—she kept a frown. She needed her ideal, however unrealistic it seemed.

She needed a god—who was eager to please. I was her idol but now, I had simply lost my means.

She wanted to live in a castle—without a care in the world. She wanted maids and a comfort that would never break. She wanted an easy life with no suffering or sacrifice. Marriage was supposed to be her escape—her paradise, her salvation and compensation for her pain. And my-love would fund her reward.

I paid. If this is what it took to make her heart break, I happily gave.

I was warned—I anticipated the heartache and was happy to let my heart break.

I wondered and hoped that one day perhaps, she will see that it was not okay to continue to take—that relationships only lasted when both parties chose to participate. I hoped that one day she would help me mend our broken faith, and restore what was lost in our family name.

That reality was simply not ready.

"Was she void of compassion?" I wondered: "was she really not aware?"

"No! Even a bad person will put up a guise—an artifice and hope it will suffice."

I decided to believe she was ignorant and brushed it aside. I had to believe. I needed something to help our love grow stronger— conviction to help me go on longer.

In belief, I would teach better; I would be kinder. I would be more patient; I would be wiser—I would not see just my own side—after all, how could she give what she did not have!

The only way I could go on was to believe she had no chance.

In belief, I tried.

In hindsight, where was the 'we'? In wanting the best for Lemon, all I served was 'me'.

Quartermaster

Now exhausted, I had lost my way. Who knew this price will be wicked to pay:

> Was I really Love?
> Did Mother tell a lie?
> Was I going to die?

> Where was all my wit—my innate ability to speak?
> Did father not raise a finer man!

I thought he did.

I was not only her lover, I had taken up the responsibility of father—and by God, I will try: This soul will not die! I would do my duty; I would do right. If I had failed as husband, I would excel as Pa.

I was eager to mend her. I was desperate to try.

I decided a more focused approach; one that I knew—one I thought was prudent and would surely bloom: I told her the truth.

The Great Depression

Lemon had just learned that while she was trying to be a good wife, the love she shared—however misunderstood, was not fairly reciprocated. In realizing she had been condescended on, she grew more bitter and angry in our already bittersweet love. She feared it was all a lie; loving a man as husband who was more interested in fixing what he perceived were her wiles.

She was right to be mad.

She battled what she thought was a lack of purpose in our marriage. And I struggled to appreciate why we were 'there' after I confessed.

For lack of established intention, the nights became tedious and unkind.

Because she won't forgive, Lemon suffered deep darkness in her sleep. Haunted by hate, she perspired hysterically—into consciousness each day:

Gasping for air, she fearfully confessed she had another nightmare.

In the day, she felt a great sting from the world, and she loathed them right back—satisfying her urgent need to attack. And in the night, she was plagued with concern, and vile bitterness. Even with great reparation there was no rest.

Lem and I had lived together for several months now. In that time, she had fired many Maids, Drivers, and other Cadre—who for one reason or the other feared she was bad news and had caught the blues. Lemon insisted these people were the problem. To make her happy; to make life easy, I would let them go—always compassionately—asking where they will go; what they will do on their own.

These people were my purpose and my passion. Out of guilt, I let Lemon have her way and let them slip.

As I bid them farewell, I shared kind prizes to help them do well; more bribe to disguise my pitiful side.

I had started to change—my tolerance grew strange. There was only so little I could accommodate. I did not see people anymore, and my values were naught.

Where people not my commission?
Was it not Lemon's simple task as wife to support that ambition?
Shall I continue to tolerate her misgivings because of my mistake?
How long would I continue to be her slave?
Shall I say sorry for another decade?

I had hurt her; I had failed her. And now, she wouldn't forgive, and I wouldn't leave.

"I would be her slave until belief".

Could we ever be partners?
When would we help make good dreams come true?
Where were the people?

Where did everybody go?

...

Nursing her hate became my full-time job—my full-time life. I stopped going to work and we suffered for that.

Worried my playful interaction with other people upset her—I stopped seeing anyone—we remained in the house.

All that was good, and a home collapsed: The walls bled from our nightmares—they whaled in the night—until their lungs were warped.

So devastating—anguish slowly eroded the rhythm of our hearts.

Lemon feared the guards and other cadre would break into the house and maltreat her because they despised her. Frightened, she always wanted me around even though she did not like me. I stayed, and suffocated in her hate.

Did Love not save us so we can save others?
Was I wrong?
Was this right?

Why couldn't I just be her Knight—a good husband, and polite—what she needed to do right.

But I gave what I thought she needed, when I thought she needed help. And she gave me what I needed to be myself:

We fed off each other's complexities until there was nothing left: "I was her savior, and she was my cry for help".

But still...

'This soul will be saved; this soul will not break,' I affirmed.
I believed in Lemon. Inside of her was Gold—inside of her
was Love. She was my child, and I loved her still.

But she was also woman, and my wife.
Why was I saddened by that?

I was now half my body mass—without smiles—before Lemon noticed I could die. And when I would see old acquaintances, they would worry.

I had brought on my defeat and perhaps deserved it. I had given all of me to her, and she stumped over it. I became the abyss I once feared she was.

In emptiness we fought; we tussled and we turned—two loud miserable gongs, aching in their bittersweet love—void of God's

Both Lemons, her chest ached and my back began to break.

My body began to collapse: there were jerks, there were sweats and there were fever spells.

In worry, or at least what I hoped was sheer concern, Lemon caught a break: she feared I was dying; she feared I'd go to waste.

In all of her regret and hatred, she knew that I loved her—and perhaps that love was the only thing left.

The first appointment with the Doctors didn't quite pay—their pointy needles and cold probes, to no avail. So I was rendered to specialists who were eager to ascertain—what ultimately, was the cause of my pain.

Wasn't this all strange:
'Love' in a hospital—bedridden; Band-Aid?

I now had a team of Doctors—me—who I thought was love; who had never been to Hospital more than a day.

They poked, and probed some more, and came up with all sorts of cerebrate flaws.

The news of my illness was contained; I did not want my siblings to know. I feared it will spawn another panel, and abhorrent bone.

It was easy—no one was there.

Electricity

Dear Lion,

What's it like to fall in Love?

Sometimes, I think it a song on a piano—a symphony with no
end or beginning. Like being there, and not knowing how you
got here—you just appeared in a song that played all day long.

What's it like to fall in love?

Love

I was now consulting with Homeland's foremost neurologist—Doctor
Avocado.

He had learned of my symptoms and took special interest.

We had great talks—he thought I was intense, and eccentric. I thought he was brilliant and polite. He also thought I had a complex mentality, and at least a balance of intriguing minds—what got him inspired. I thought he was kind.

He referred me to a psychologist when I would not accept his diagnosis.

Doctor Date—after a chat, thought I suffered abysmal depression. I asked how a mental condition could manifest so devastatingly in physical state. He explained rationally, I obeyed.

Doctor Date described my state as something that was not trivial—a genuine health condition—he called it. He insisted I was really ill—with real symptoms and reassured me it was not a sign of weakness or something I could snap out of by 'pulling myself together'.

He wanted to know the cause of my deep sadness, and eventually advised on a course of medication I would not take.

For a third opinion I telephoned 'Georgia'. Angel Angelo answered, and scheduled appointments with accomplished Specialists. Along with inquiry, he arranged for and sent flight tickets. Angelo loved me dearly, and feared for my health.

Through the rack of emotions, I did not waver in a set resolve to love my wife. But I had now become weak, and lousy with it: at times when I had had it, "I packed a bag and grabbed it!". And when I left, it hurt Lemon in her chest.

We retuned to darker nights—our-love, bitter and black: you could taste it in the air—like soft, thin pills that forced their way in the belly of your mouth.

We were dying, and everyone who existed with us in that space could not stand the place.

She had communicated severe chest pain and started to see Doctor Date. And when her heart wasn't aching, she hated me for making it break.

She detested me for inviting her into a place she was despised.

In the depth of her bitterness, she would communicate regret. She would then follow with sober apology on her knees—begging me to forgive. As soon as I did—in another feat of venting rage, she would reveal the same.

She would lie in bed all day with a claim she was in pain—my love, responsible for her ail. She had stopped going to work, and her illness freed her form her wifely chores. She spent her days in front of screens and wallowed in her absorption of unrequited fantasy.

I stood and watched her struggle to breathe in her sourness and self-pity: "if it were a thing that glorified God, I would die for her". But I didn't want her to die for me, not like this. Not full of hate, and licentious waste.

I wondered,

> "If I went away, will she be OK?
> Will she learn to forgive, and allow her heart to live?"

We discussed the odds.

My-love wouldn't budge. Every time it came up, she snapped out of her wallow and illness, as if she were on swanky drugs.

Lemon would only come alive when I told her I was done—when she thought I was set—and feared she wasn't the one. Like a jolt from a defibrillator, it was only then she took rambunctious breaths—when she felt I was near my end. In what appeared to be her need to survive, a decaying girl suddenly found her bloom and bounce, and capped Edwardian courtesans.

It was clear then—Lemon had life in her but chose not to share.

> *What withered effort on a man who just wanted*
> *to love, and be freed from his wrong.*

I decided I would no longer be her excuse for death.

I would set my young beauty free—to live a life without a lie; one I hoped she wouldn't have to die.

I sat on the thought for a while; the notion of nostalgia made me cry. I wondered what I'd miss; what it would feel like to lose a lovers kiss; what it meant to loose a wife who used to be sister;

What it meant to care for them as family; as friend—what I now believed was the beginning of our end. With it, I hoped my promise to love and care for her would stand.

I thought of her reaction to my reflection in a thousand dimensions. The more I thought about it, the less it mattered.

Love is not mathematical or strategic. It does not plot its way. It's a thought that sinks into our hearts—a truth that cannot be wrestled with and won't break.

Love is a tearjerker once understood, a jubilant exhale after a long wait—a relief from the pain—your guarantee of free reign. Love is like fresh air—not forceful; does not need to be begged, convinced or pleased. Love is alive—ready, willing and able to give, believe-in, and love all things.

'Truelove' loved Lemon indeed.

We were alive—only for a while—and when she wasn't scared, the passion went dead.

Haysia

Dear Lion,

Once upon a time, I knew a spirit called Haysia. She was beauty and autumn. She bloomed in the spring, chimed in the winter, and danced in the summer.

But in the autumn she was sublime; Love's tethered child—she never frowned. She filled the streets with her dark brown sheets and soft golden leafs.

The winter wrote her odes; her good nature was pure and gold. Her treats were wise, and her perfection, kind.

She was a dance I loved to dance, a song I loved to sing.

She was a dream I loved to dream.

One day she'll be reality.

Love,
Lion

She was my most sacred dream, and I shared her with Lemon when life was not so tragic.

These were dark times—whiles of dire melancholy and grave illness in the night. We were sick and alone. Our only hope was what was left of our dying home.

In her desperation for life, she remembered that dream.

She whispered a soft thought in our aching misery, "Haysia... 'Away from it all'—the stress, the pain, the flaws."

What wouldn't I do for her?

Even though indulgent, I was sad she had turned the purest of dreams into revelation for our prodigious need to be free. But Lemons without love wouldn't understand what woe desperation had towed.

I urged my-love, "it will be folly to run! How far could we dash from Love's justice or Hatred's woeful claws—where they not in us?"

She insisted it would make her happy. I wanted her to be happy. I needed to be forgiven. I was eager to save her; I was desperate to try. Without sound mind, great power or true love, I made a way for us to break away.

Lemon loved the thought of living in Haysia. It gave her life.

Immediately, we found lands to live in and sought their Lords to pay lease. I would work in the day as an English Instructor and she would learn the local tongue. And in the evenings, she would discover herself and I would master Haysian depths.

I wanted Lemon to learn who she was more than I wanted to be "Love". I felt it was my responsibility to help her blossom into my perception of her best self, and soak up good depths. She had spent her joy on sadness, and her mornings had become the grime of the night. And my love had become her pain, and meager aid.

I was going to leave it all behind: for me, for her; for love—or whatever I thought it was.

Capital

Pepper lived in the capital.
When she learned I was coming, she insisted I stayed with her. I obliged happily.

She was a breath of fresh air from the moment we met at Father's funeral. She was dark, lovely and had shiny white teeth. Before I learned she was my half-sister, I thought she was the girl of my dreams. Pepper was intelligent and wise, chubby and kind—she had a heart of a million moons; like Haysia, her love was never blue.

We've been close ever since, and her arms were quite the retreat.

We talked about everything the night I arrived—the weather, songs and stars. She was truly my blood—my sister, 'Truelove'. I told her this story, and it made her worry.

She feared for my heart, and prayed earnestly for my head.
She didn't judge me—she loved me as Lemon instead.

I was comfortable—and in her love, all of my symptoms disappeared: I did not twitch, the headaches stopped, and I started to remember who I was.

I would turn-in that night, and wake with a terrible fever. It will keep me from my visa, and two sweet and sour fruits from Haysia.

Beyond Haysia

I breathed a deep sigh: I feared a life in exile with my wife. Before my visit to the Capital, I would fantasize about leaving a very comfortable, independent and well settled-in Lemon in Kapan while I made my way to another state, hoping she wouldn't need me; knowing she wouldn't wait.

I reveled in the thought that she needed my ability to help her, more than she needed me. Perhaps I thought too much of myself.

"We were in a yolkless relationship," she said—one that was alien, and perhaps taboo: as if two siblings preyed on the notion of romance, and failed.

I said my farewell to the Capital that day—and thanked her for my stay. I hopped on a plane, and soon was nigh.

We landed at night—the taxi was slow. Once again, I was alone and felt the cold.
Lemon called to check in, and the tremors set back in. The twitching was deeper and my bones felt weaker.

That night, before she engaged me, she took in deep breaths—
and asked if my body shook in Pepper's care. I hesitated before I
answered while she held her breath. I knew response would hurt her.
So I danced around the truth but eventually confessed.

She wept. I held her in my arms as she cried, and as I did—my body
shook harder, and she cried louder. She thought now—she was killing
me and when she would try to break away for my sake, I would hold
her tight for hers.

I wasn't sad. I just wasn't alive.

Haysia was now a lost dream—like the other Apples on the chilly tree.

Dear Haysia,

Sweet little girl...
I'm sorry you were belittled, and thought a tool.

I still think of you—your warm winters, and cold springs.

You're forever in my dreams.

Dear Lion,

What if we left?

Love,
Child

Till Death do us Part

Ever wondered about death; his color, her depth?
Ever wonder about her consciousness?
She must be alive to take a life.
Or is she a man—could he be my wife?

I was pushing up daisies; all of what was purpose in me was beat:

I was not leading. I was not feeding the poor; I wasn't helping to make good dreams come true. I was rather unsure.

I was not a reason to love. And because I was not serving, I was dying.

I thought I deserved it. So, I let myself expire.

In death, on one of those long drives, on one of those long nights, I remembered what life was about; one simple task: to help make good dreams come true.

I dashed home, and in what Lemon thought was a spur, I asserted we be apart.

Tree of Life

3

All night

Dear Lion,

If you were here, I wouldn't write:
We'll talk all night and I'll stare at your heart.

Maybe I'll do more than that.

Dear Lion,

If you were here, I wouldn't write—
I wouldn't think, I wouldn't type.
I'd rub my mind between your brows and make my way into
your heart.

Dear Lion,

If you were here, I wouldn't sleep; I wouldn't eat, I wouldn't drink.
I would kiss you softly on your cheek, and bow meekly to the
sole of your feet.

Dear Lion,

If you were here, I wouldn't write—
I'd stay here with you, all night.

Love,
Lion

Compassion

I have heard compassion is forged from pity and a generous concern for ones seemingly awful self.

In context, what I learned was right. Georgia would be kind.

Dear Love,

Yours is a tenderness that concocts change—a love that is true; Truelove that is good.

Don't stop,
Lion

Georgia's fairest Apple picked me up from the Airport in his new CC. He swooped in like a fairytale protagonist—eager to please. Let me tell you how I met Angel Angelo:

It was the winter after father. I had entered new lands by means of admission into university.

Central Winton was dull, but "The Bull" was exciting and new. International students would assemble carousingly, a week before "Fresher's" were due.

That night, I contemplated the thought to attend: "for sure it was another shallow trend". I was quiet, and didn't mind my confidence.

Eventually, I cruised to the big hall, and in no time, they were playing my-song.

Under the disco lights, it appeared it was Angel Angelo's too. He came over, and at the end of the night his friends were mine. We remained best friends over the next four years—and after university, agreeable brethren.

Georgia's Angel was doing well.

I wonder now,

Did I let myself suffer to understand her?

I had given me up to be with Lemon, and instead of strengthening her
when I thought her weak; I had fallen flat to her feet.

Was this sacrifice or stupidity?
Was this love—when did I get it wrong?

I had sunk into my death or ascended into her life.

However I saw it, I had made a big sacrifice.
I needed compassion.

Dear Lion,

I do not understand my joy—
It is full, and overflowing.
I have found a peace that does not ask why, and I know won't
ever die.

I have fallen at your feet: I know your whiskers and your truth.
I know your hair and love your sneer.

Your heart is not faint. It is Lion, and all so dear.
Your love is a loud roar—she shakes the earth and the skies. They
tremble at the sound of your cry.

And when you breathe: settling winds—that hold my mast, and
set my sail to lasting peace.
Sail Lion...

I am in love with Beauty and a Beast.

And when she cries, she fills the Nile. My Lion brings plenty
to these parched lands.

My Lion is alive. My Lion is Love—
Love's 'Truelove'

Angel Angelo hadn't changed a bit. He was the same ace with a gleaming heart. What a comforting sight, and well cherished delight. I loved him—it felt easy to be in his company.

We talked. That was good.

I didn't tell him much. But the little he heard, got him concerned. I wanted him to love her no matter what; so I curbed my tale and gave it new end.

I decided to take it easy in Georgia; we visited the bars and threw soirees to sooth broken hearts. Angelo was kind.

Other times I took long walks and talked to God. And when I felt strong enough, I visited the shops.

My symptoms had abated, and in time I was full and well. And so, the good Angel insisted I stayed.

Lemon and I had started talking again. I had related with a few of her aunties just before I left. They advised we stay apart, citing it was for the best and in time we'd learn our better selves. Albeit their plea, we still sought affection from one another to heal.

Eagle

Dear Lion,

Your love teaches a kindness and consideration that makes me
noble.

Love

Restless in her mother's nest—a young and quite eager Lemon would
seek out our redemption and ask for help. Soon, she would write to
inform me of her travel to Matakar's south. There, she would meet a
great teacher; a man I would come to love as cleric and dear friend.

In his home, we will be taught to pray.

Pastor Mongo was a simple man. He had four sensational children and an inspiring wife.

His children were their names:

King
Apple
Love
Obey

They all knew God's Spirit and had learned how to pray.

When we were younger, Lemon liked to talk about the Church. To her, it was a place she grew up. She spoke about the Pastors like they were her idols. And when she spoke, she wore a reminiscent smile.

She worshiped them—they became her 'father'—and the Church, her cornerstone.

At her depth, she will run there for help.

Mango's was a catholic cornerstone.

When Lemon called, she would hand over the phone and in time I would learn his children, and treasure the meanings of their names; I would learn a beautiful mother, and admire the nature of her beguiling mate.

They counseled and coached us in love. Our hearts succumbed, and finally I yielded to Pastor Mango's call:

I would catch the next flight to Homeland's South, to be with my wife.

A conversation with Corinthians

My family was back, and callously pleased with my separation from Lemon.

Some clamored, "I dodged a bullet" while some playfully threatened to abandoned me if I let her back in.

If only they knew the whole tale—Lemon and I were quite the same. But family is family—so I was without blame.

All was as mother left it. I had missed my sisters; my children—quite terribly, and was deeply heartened they were back.

But in my gratitude, I was dissatisfied:

Does love abandon?
Is love not wild?
Does love leave a man behind?

I saw Lemon clearer than anyone. I did not like her—but I loved her. She was my family. I believed in family and I believed in love—love never fails!

I couldn't tell my Apples—not today.

In transit, we talked about everything; we confessed the complexity of our entirety—these stories now told. Where there was hurt, there was weeping. And where there was pain, what I hoped was forgiveness.

She shared Bible scripture with me every day and in time, showed great change. We acknowledged our wrongs and slowly, we loved.

...

Homeland's sturdy Boeing taxied her southern runway at eight. Lemon was there to pick me up. She had sparkles in her eyes, and was pleased and surprised: I had gained much weight, and was quite awake. I gave her a hug, and asked how she was: she was thin and looked quite pale.

We hurried into her taxi as we swiftly made our way.

I missed her.

In reverence that night, we settled into heart and spirit matters.

In the morning, I thanked Pastor Mango for his warm welcome.

Pastor Mango and wife encouraged us to pray every day, and reassured us all will be OK; "God is the author of marriage and in Him, the key to its success" they confessed.
Lemon listened completely. I had never seen her hope and believe so deeply. She was full of faith, and joy and promise.

I wanted to try with that woman.

We stayed a few more days, and we learned to pray.

Lemon promised she would keep up the practice when we returned to our home. I assured the Mango's I would do the same.

This powerful Pastor and his faithful wife insisted our marriage depended on that.

Before Lem and I left, we shared hopeful hugs, and exchanged enlightened kisses.

Life became simple; life was our marriage—and if knowing God and learning to pray was what it took to save it, then God and prayer we became.

Home Sweet Home

Home

The fabric of the walls was a frightening thought; what these walls have seen, who these walls have been.

These walls have taught us, and bore us. They have carried us, and cared for us.

In 'Love' they have grown taller, stronger. But 'our love' has shattered virtue. For our feet and hearts have left this house.

Hollow Sticks

Home was a pile of wreck; un-catered for, she turned to earth.

Rebuilding would take everything from us, and its toll.

Our families started to murmur; we were back in town, and Lemon was in my home.

I thought it appropriate to assemble the Apples, and share newfound sight; Homeland tradition demanded it was right.

We engaged the prospects, and agreed to set a date.

Meanwhile, we began to pray just as Pastor Mango and his dear wife had taught us. We prayed in Spirit for hours each day—just as they did; like we said we would.

Would we not be fools to show weakness in battle?

And this was a holy war; a combat for the immortality of our love—however destructive it appeared it was.

Through prayer, we would replace every element of destruction with God's eternal restoration—I believed all would be well.

And all was well.

With prayer, we ate the word of God, and it lifted us up.

It truly worked.

But Lemon was still afraid, and her nightmares loomed again. She thought of our separation, and was bitter about the ease with which my family encouraged it. She wanted to be missed; she needed to know that she was married into a family that won't resist—a family that will not celebrate when we were separate. She wanted to feel safe and loved; she needed to feel welcomed and adored.

I saw these things, and so I prayed that God's love would make it easier to forgive.

In love I sat with my kin, urging them to open their hearts and be glad—to show good faith, and love for Heaven's sake.

They shared their concerns. To which I proffered understanding to alleviate their fears. With God's word, I helped to settle their troubles, and slowly, Truelove took charge: His children would unwind.

Lemon will not meet me halfway. She insisted she still was despised, and all the Apples lied.

We will suffer again.

Suffering

What an odd sound.

Dear Lion,

What does it take to be Love? And if long-suffering is a characteristic, what must one suffer for—and for how long?

I understand a suffering from compromise and hardship. I understand a selfish sacrifice to survive.

What I cannot bear is suffering from foolishness; an unkind agony dealt from a lack of submission to lessons learned.

For suffering as a function of this calamity is not just travail, it is madness and an ignorance that is not bliss or an excuse, and certainly isn't cute;

"A recklessness I fear—not only kills you but destroys everyone around you".

Love is not foolish—is it? Love is not ignorant; love is not hateful or lazy, Love is not proud.

I would suffer for long with humble imperfection.
I would die for a love I knew was true; a love I knew was good.
I would go without water and without food,
I would live under a bridge, in the depths of rainy waters—in the arms of a loving Lion.

But that's me.

Dear Lion,

Tell me what you need. Please ready my heart to give.

Lemon had not kept her word. She had stopped praying.

And when she stopped, I urged her to start. In hurt, I asked, "Love, if you knew that all it took to keep us up was to drink water from a well, will you not drain the well?"

There was no noise, showing love was now a simple matter: *desperation to drain a well of living water.*

If this was all it took to show love; to show interest, then my-love—I feared, did not love me. My-love became a horse forced to the stream—she will drink no water. She will die a thirsty steed.

A Thirsty Horse

She had stopped.

I was deeply saddened by that. This woman had urged me strongly to stay and fight in her desperation to redeem us. "Prayer was the last piece of string our relationship hung from," she said. I believed her because I thought we were dead. So here I am, with one thought: what does this woman really want? —It couldn't possibly be us.

To secure us was made simple:

Love
Pray
Forgive

She struggled with love, prayer and forgiveness. And I struggled to understand.

Lemon allowed resentment to make her weak and sick again. Constantly drowning in what she feared was our lot, we were back to Hates woeful claws.

Silly me, I hoped still.

A meeting of cynics

The date we set was due.

We met in a house not too far from our living room. Dinner boiled in the kitchen while the oven cooked. The table was set—we would talk first before dessert.

Our matter would now become a debate, and open case.

...

That morning, Lemon and I made love. She was nervous and afraid.

The day before, Lemon met with her Aunties and Apples. I had a meeting with hers and later on, encountered mine.

As we dined at night, we shared nothing about daytime; what felt like the essence of trust had been misplaced. Soon, we would learn the details.

The meeting commenced;

Present were:

> Three of Mother's daughters and an
> Aunty Apple—all four struggled
> to attend.

> Lemon invited Carrot and three
> lovely friends—together, they
> were Lemon's defense.

Flares were exchanged—heated banter, turned into flames. Fire that will soon consume all we had worked hard to attain. Lemon was asked if she felt afraid—if she felt my home was unsafe—how they twisted our words like snakes. My-love denied me, and the panel dealt the same:

> Lemon will return to her mother, and we will go our separate ways.

In what appeared to be a need to please, Lemon acknowledged and agreed.

What a sight: *my Lemon in Apples paradise.* How she always wanted to fit in.

An agenda to inform of Godly insight had
now become the Devils delight.

I would learn later that the meetings had before we sat, had been to secure this rather odd and shifty plight; Lemon had shared thoughts that galvanized these shocking questions, and these brave Apples had swayed Lemon to correspond—knowing what she would want;

"The thrills of Homeland court."

The party rejoiced at the outcome—all but Carrot. However dire and disturbing her prior allegation, her moue was genuinely low.

We ate amid fake smiles—a meal to complement Lemon's guile. My sister's and I would fall out again; Lemon spilled venom much to that dismay.

The crowd dispersed, I was alone—my only companion, a tall black road.

I attended that meeting with a trying wife, three absolving sisters and a soft red heart. I left with a broken soul, and a very slow stroll. I would walk for miles to my empty home.

Revelry

I was alone, and believed I was a free man. I wondered the streets quite literally: I would get down from a moving car and just walk distances to enjoy intention. My nights were merry—the crowd and company, a mighty treat. I attended concerts at The Great Apple's Happy Park, and dined with stars at Homeland's heart, and just enjoyed the sites.

My life was my own again; I was free from Lemon—

Heartbreak had finally done us part.

How to Write a Precise Truth

The emotions that followed were unclear: I simply was—with and without joy. I had become used to being married; the frequent sex, gourmet foods, and the good old 'Irish cuddle'—*these dull nights left me choked up and under the moon.*

In time we exchanged letters—where she tried to explain what happened in calamitous meeting. I read. She complained she didn't think I supported or protected her when my sisters affirmed their concerns. I read. And it was just that—I read.

Soon, all the Aunties and Apples at the table, saving her from said "beastly concern" would disappear. Perhaps they dug deeper into the matter and learned it was too intricate to bear. Perhaps they simply didn't care.

Now Lemon was left alone.
My darling: a paradox of sophistication, beauty and true malice; a nostalgic enigma, my bittersweet dream.

A Terribly Vexing Concern

We had had it with marriage counselors—had we not learned enough? We had no supporters—even the local priests advised we get a quiet divorce. All abandoned the impression of us. We were faux pas, a predilection not to last—an item for a joke.

No one believed in us—no one but Orange saw a yolk.

Orange

Orange grew up in the Garden of Spring. A mighty Spirit dwelled within. In Spring, there was no temptation—just Love, and an enchanting sweet-smelling fruit.

Ms. Orange would run on the bright green grass at dawn, and swim in the pure blue stream at twilight. And at night, Love would teach her His charge. A studious student she was—cleverer than anyone, she excelled at all Love's chores.

Love had faith in her, and He put her to test: He released His Spirit upon her, and sent her forth—into the world.

What fine revelation she was—bright and about, she spread the joy of the teachings Love taught. She taught of a God, Lion of a proud nation—Beauty of an exuberant tribe. Wherever she traveled she was renowned—and her nature was always sound.

She was 'Truelove', and she was good—and her word was a trembling remedy to life's grey and seeming confusions.

She counseled, "what a soul!"—such vigor, and relentless hope. She retorted a concise and precise understanding to every "but..." and "what if" and anger and disbelief. She was complete in her judgment, and powerful in her mind. She was very fund of me and I loved her dearly. So, I listened.

Lemon and I will try again.

This time, Orange advised we do things properly:

We would gather all the Uncles, Mothers, Fathers and Apples—for an "Introductory" banquet—as we should have before we eloped. There, we will affirm our intentions to wed traditionally, without leaving subject open for discussion. After "Introduction", we would wed 'Traditionally', where I would pay Lemon's "Bride price", as is customary—and finally, we will tie the knot faithfully—in the presence of our God and family—what Homeland natives refer to as "the Church wedding".

Furthermore, we will establish true purpose in our affair: I would love her devoutly, and she would care affectionately.

"What fine entertainment our relationship would make on a Hollywood screen" I joked. Lemon would laugh, thinking I took nothing seriously. Perhaps that's what love's about: not taking life or death so seriously:

> Dancing in a crisis,
> Praising in a fire,
> Sleeping soundly in a storm

Once again, I would journey to Carrot's keep to sweep my dear wife off her feet.

Quite an affair—the nature of their relationship: this mother, this girl. Having loved them both, I feared the cocktail of emotion that stirred. Simultaneously, I had come to understand they were of the same kind, and had been through similar grime; they stuck together all the time.

They seemed to be a variation of clever that was more agenda-full than simple. Nevertheless, it was clear they just wanted their perception of the best.

I would smile as they laughed at my cavalier slant to Homeland culture, and giggle in support when they called me white-man.

I thought very little of it. Whatever my thoughts were, I cared for them still.

Time passed as we made preparations to celebrate.

Meanwhile my boy—Carrot's Cocopine—remained in stale state while The Great Apple Schools flourished, and built a good name. Carrot did not keep her end of the deal; Lemon did what she thought was elite. Once again, both mother and daughter cast a shade too grey to age. Carrot's and mine became an affair turned cold, and I lingered with Lemon, hanging from a knackered thread of hope.

Why bother I thought.

Why struggle to be here when you don't care?

Cocopine was abandoned, and on his own—and I was ashamed I couldn't come to his aid. I had failed to keep the promise I made.

In the frailty of faith, I entrusted the engine of his dream to who I believed was his family. And now, I didn't know if their efforts were futile, or I had been deceived. I was letdown completely.

I would have to answer to him—my son—six feet and four inches of broken dream; my son, who I had promised to give everything.

> *But how could we treat him this way?*
> *How could we pretend everything was OK?*

Yes—Lemon had explained, and Carrot danced around self-proclaimed faith. But how could we plan a wedding when Cocopine's heart was heavy? How would we justify expense of ceremony when we had failed to feed a young man God's glory? Our priorities were misplaced—it seemed.

As I explained, Lemon could not see—but instead believed I had grown cold feet.

Advocating strongly we use whatever cash we had to support Cocopine's dream, I had chosen her younger brother over 'we'.

And if you have read up to this page, you must know what banquet of ill fate laid in wait:

We slipped into bittersweet, and our trembling love—truly grew cold feet.

Living with Death

"Enthusiasm" quickly turned into death and her famous regret. 'Forgiveness' didn't care. No lessons were learned. Life was gout, and 'truelove', without.

We broke the walls of the house.

Dear Lion,

I have heard: "the worst thing you can say to your spouse is, 'I regret marrying you'."

I took it simply, and thought to myself, 'there must be worse things'.

The next time Lemon communicated regret, I lost interest.

In spite of my subjective sedition, Lemon feared the thought of a rowdy event that celebrated our affair—she feared the energies; she feared a world that sneered.

How much fear could we entertain? How much hate was left in our veins?

O Lord,
It's getting late...

The greater light, the lesser light,
and the constellation of stars

Still we remained in this place. We tussled and turned, and even though we ached, we were quieter in our bangs. We settled to read the word of God together—this manual of marriage, this book of true love. With it, our minds were slowly renewed. Our fights were more—constructive. With every perceived destructive word, we would eventually take the time to explain its origin and offer sincere apology to atone for our suffering.

We shared our deep dark thoughts on each other, were I confessed I thought she was narcissist. I further explained I read the characteristics and thought she fit the tricks, and even teased that her ring was a depiction of said description. She confessed she thought I was callous and had no real interests; a 'truelove' mascot—with no real faith—all I did was entertain.

Where I laughed at her confessions, she cried at mine. It appeared my thoughts were too tedious for her to try.

As a gesture of good faith and a commitment to stay, I took her white-gold diamond ring and avowed the stones:

The greater light, the lesser light, and the constellation of stars;

Praying the shiny diamonds on the outer rim: "the greater light," *the Sun*; the black sparkly diamonds on the inner rim: "the lesser light," *the moon*—and the big, black diamond in the middle, *the constellation of stars.*

I touched her chest, and prayed God's
eternal light into her depths.

When I hoped the season would change, winter became mundane. The nights were harder on us, and the days, a gat away. We had entered a bitter state again—as if it never left. Its acid filled the air and my trembling began again. This time—much stronger than the last, I commanded the sickness out—as if I knew I had the power to; like it were my inheritance and truth. I lay my hand on her chest, and spoke life into her breath.

I insisted we fill ourselves with God's love, "a Lions word".

Lemon only got sicker and weaker with every attempt to wake her.

She started to fear her death.
When she was not haunted in her sleep, she spent the days in dreams and we bickered in-between.

...

Words

I have heard, "it takes maturity to write"; to capture a precise truth; a potent plight, a humble paradise.

How belittling it must be to describe existence with words:

Are words ever enough?

So we don't write, or produce prose. We etch our souls, and inscribe our woes. We create poetry—proverbs of an ancient art, words that never go out of sight.

Lemon's words broke loves spell. Eager to attack, she released a bitter fire that chaperoned torment. It burned me as well.

Words...

Words are a catalyst for behavior, a trigger for death. In a sentence, we spell our names. In another, we crumble in hate.

Words beat us, as they raise us. Words give life, or execute us.

Words are a comfort; they seduce us.

Lemon spoke her last words in a quarrel that started in perspiring regret. Eager to kill, she let his venom spill. I saw in her—the depths of her ill: an echo of desperation, a need for a pill, agonizing screams from her suffering—a bitter need to be free.

In fear and anger, she declared I was not—and denounced me of who I was.

This raging bull—I feared I had seen—but now revealed, it was nothing like I dreamed. Revolting and big chested—fully shown: scattered—horns sharpened, ready to dethrone.

> Tortured by 'Truelove', he thundered like a throbbing Beast, falling out of a deeply dark abyss— scratching on his insides, as if he were petrified.
>
> A deadly fiend; scared and terrified, anxious and proud. I saw her in him; pale skinned, and fair— waiting to excel.
>
> I took a stance to wrestle the beast— "now it was out, now was my chance."
>
> Out of **her**, he stood to charge. He burned bigger and redder—all that was light, was night—and these flames burdened fright. The curtains caught the fire; Anguish began her choir.

I was out of love, and full of rage—intent to tame,
busting out with pain.

The beast charged into me, and I pierced its heart
with my whetted Hollow sticks.

In fatality, we fell apart.

Bleeding in decay, we both gazed—through the
fire—"look what a mess we've made".

I took one final look at her, as I burned in Lemons
spell, and prayed she wouldn't die as well.

'Truelove' lingered in the depths of hate to save that little girl.

Her words continued till the walls were rubble. My
deep dark Lemon had finally been ruined".

I let her exhaust her hate, and made our-love its bait.

I finally saw her: "I was her father" and she hated me.
"I was her mother"; every mistake she thought she made—the
reason she never forgave.

I let the fire burn us until our hearts gave.
In the ashes of our hurt, is where we both laid.

I finally knew her:

We never fought again.

In the middle of our fiery exchange, we forgot to tend to the pot—that by now had caught a flame.

Absorbed by hate and true disdain—the fire spread until the neighbors began to cry out our names.

In the center of our living, the smoke began to rise—choking up our insides. The fire had spread; all we could do was save our breath.

But we tried—we did what we could to extinguish it from the inside. However now, it was too late; all that we built was lost in hate.

We watched from the outside as the fire raged—looking at each other—thinking, "what a mess we've made".

Without words, we slowly walked away—apart, the saddest moment of our lives.

Dear Lion,

Before you came, I was waiting to become.

I died once—and in death, I forgot who I was.
I died for another; Love emptied my soul to save her.

In my heart, it's Truelove I remember: "The Lion of the tribe of Judah".

It is You I have become—Your love, the only one.
It is You that completes me. It is You that has broken me.

I am yours faithfully—truly,

Love

The fire burned the whole place—with it, our hurt and pain.

She disappeared into the smoke.
And I remained: the heart of winter.

Time passed—a few years and a half...

We made no contact.

Death and Decision

Dear Lion,

You are Beauty in the morning; the freshness of the dew, the breeze over these humble waters, and salt under the moon.

I escape into you—my safe place—and when the world is safe, inside of you is my dwelling place.

I invite you into the heart of my hollow sticks, and ask that you to take charge.

Fill me up Love—don't ever go away.

Yours truly,
Love

In the cold, I knew what I was, and who I wanted to be.

I was "my love" —who walked away from me.
I asked Abba Father if I could save us—then paused to wonder if
that was a good prayer: For how could I save us when I was freezing
in my rot?

I wanted to be more than me; more thank Lemon, or Hollow Sticks.

I wanted to be Truelove, enact God's word.
All I wanted to be was His son.

So, I lay down everything—all the rage inside of me.

A Silver Queen

When I was a boy, I dreamed of a little girl: Hers was the most magnificent eyes I'd ever seen.

She was 'Truelove' and a Queen. She was white, and she was gold; like sunrays through Linen from an open window.

When I closed my eyes, she was there—a big spirit, a little child—always guiding, always mild.

She loved me, I could tell. It was composed in the might of her hair.

Every time I met "her", she would whisper to me, "not her" —as if a fetus were selecting a womb to be, Edel would whisper, "she's not Queen" —every time I was in love, or thought I was.

She was kind, gentle and playful. She loved life, and loved Love.

At night, I would watch her comb her hair, and then her spirit would tuck me into bed.

As we lay, I listened to the softness of her breath, and felt the warmth in the ventricle of her chest.

A nameless spirit, I called her Edel—she was white and she was gold; "a pure spirit with nowhere to go".

She was a blessing, and she was hope; an old story I never told.

Now, I'm glad you know.

Affinity: An Infinite Consciousness

Good Morning!

My favorite
prayer, a
beautiful song,
and single line of
praise.

Good morning
Abba Father;
Good morning
Truelove;
Good morning
Lion!

Good morning,
Homeland!!
Fairest and
darkest of the
Matakar lands!
Heartbeat of a
continent and the
seasoned seas!

"Good morning,
good Lady; good
morning dear
Lamb"

I had finally learned that my love was not enough for Lemon; not enough to see us; not enough to please us. Ours was a depth deeper than me, deeper than the oceans and the seas.

I have learned a love taller than the trees, wider than the oceans and the galaxies—a Love that fills; a love that believes, a love that strengthens and gainfully completes.

I have learned a Lion's love, much bigger than me—Truelove, living inside of me.

I gave her that love:

A love that was simple, a love that was true, a love that did not need or hope to forgive—a love that did not expect, and would not repent: a love that simply loved—without regret.

Truelove Tree

4

Silver Winters That
Melt into Spring

I married Lemon in the warmth of an Apple summer.

We got on our knees and said a prayer that would last a while.

I married Lemon because I wanted to give her a home—a safe place I thought she would grow; a place she would learn she was Love and she was Gold; a place where our love would never grow old.

Crude and complex, I broke up with her to prove a sad theory, and cache a forged regret.

Each breakup broke her—for better,
Each breakup broke her—for worse.

Each breakup broke me—for better,
Each breakup broke me—for worse.

We would eventually break into Beauty, and would materialize 'Truelove'—that which originally was designed for us.

We died in the chill of a Lemon winter and the fire of venomous grief.

Lemon grew up in my care and I grew up with Lemon; "Mother and Father," we were.

Her mother placed her in my arms and told me to raise her.
But how could I raise a grown woman?

Truelove did not appear by my might or power—or by the complexity of my intellect—or passion of my foolishness.

It was a simple trust: "a let go, and let Love". All that was misunderstood became clear: "we were meant to be here".

I was supposed to love her; I was supposed to care. We were supposed to suffer—all that was, went well. 'Truelove' was simply taking her time until I found myself.

I created Lemon, by feeding her imperfect love—love that insisted on its way; love that judged, and never quite absolved.

She had the same look in her eyes—what I saw when I saw that boy: the ache in Cocopine's gaze; a longing for a Father's touch; a hope for 'Abba Father's' love.

All Lemon needed was love; a philanthropic drug—a wonder that never ceased: a Lion's love; true love—we all need:

A love that takes the pain away, and makes us available and willing to forgive: a love that makes it possible for 'our imperfect-love' to live.

Dear Lion,

Tonight I wept.
I wept because I love you, and I've learned to love myself.

Love,
Me

In between broken dreams—I wondered who truly was the fiend:
Tyrant and Tutor, was I ever Love?

In order for us to live, 'our love' gave, and let "Truelove" live.

So that just as a young cub grew, Truelove will finally find her bloom.

The Love Bundle

It starts with faith—trust that there is a little love inside of you, belief that casts the fear away.

Through faith, a little love starts to grow. Faith makes 'a little' strong, and quite bold. Strength gets stronger. Stronger gets bigger, and grows little toes, and feet. Feet fit to stand; tall as a tree—a tree with an apple, and Adam's heart.

So 'Abba Father' gave her a little love—the least of His affection. So that a little will become a lot of Love in her, and eventually, all of her: A little love bigger than her—a big Love, bigger than me.

A Lion and a Lamb

Dear Lion, I had a dream.

It was about a girl who was only seventeen.

Every night, she danced in the center of a Grand Ball room. And when she danced, she lit the place.

Every time she danced the crowd would part, the room disappeared and the constellation filled the space.

Everyone watched in awe, as she danced. She smiled while they gazed, and slowly waltzed the night away. She loved to dance—she didn't care for the attention, awe or romance.

She danced with the moon, sun and stars—she danced with Love, and danced for joy.

And every night, it was the same.

One night, a gentleman from out of town walked into the room and saw her dance. He swanned to her, and asked her for her hand.

He was the moon and stars, the sparkle in her eyes.

And through the night, they had their chance.

In the day he slipped away.

Dawn dusked; night returned, and the Ball was grand again—
and so was the town's grandiose Beauty. She glided in like every
other night—delicate and delight.

No one would dare touch her, or walk up to her.

Like the night before, the crowd would part, and she would begin
her heart. Only this time she couldn't; she didn't know how—it
appeared her will had failed.

All she remembered was a tango with the strong-chinned man;
her last romance. She tried—and when she couldn't, she cried.
Her sun and moon had left her heart.

The party gathered—and in time, filled the space. Soon they
began to swing at cavalier pace.

A star was forgotten; she began to wilt away.

Now in the corner, she stood still—and watched as she became ill. The sky and the clouds faded to gloom, and what once was bright, was filled with night.

First, her warmth escaped, and then grace—she calmly exhaled. Her soul leaked from her peek, and tricked from cheek to cheek. She was dying, and death was she.

Her body turned to dust, and the old place began to rust.

Her death would haunt the town, and leave the grounds a deserted land.

The Ballroom had lost its grand. And what once was grand had vastly turned to sand.

The land suffered and was without rain.
And this place, once a beautiful space, became a foul site—such ugly fate.

One day, a hand from the open space, reached into this ugly place.

"He" put his finger in the sand, and dug the dirt from under the land. In the soil, he laid a star—a seed of profound need:

The skies sent the rains over the earth. The sun and moon pushed out regret.

What was death, and full of dirt, was now well—and in good health.

He was green, a Nile and King—a leaf, like nothing you've ever seen. And from his stalk, **she** sprung up—in love; from out of the earth and into the heavens her petals spread, and relaxed in the clouds.

She was bold, and beautiful—wise, and white delight.

All the people gathered to see—what a Queen she was indeed.

In the sun, she smiled. In the moon, she danced—and seduced a crowd who craved the chance.

And when she came, she brought the rain.
All that was dead blossomed again.

Little white Flower, come out to play.
Bless my heart and Homeland again.

I realized I was the strong-chinned man who danced and left—leaving his love with dour regret.

It was me all along. I was the one filled with grief; doubt that made me bittersweet and eventually a fiend.

I was Lemon, and had lost my love. I was the one who needed a father; who needed to belong. It was I who needed love.

I invited her into a world that wasn't real—a place I could assess her ill, and give a love I thought would heal. I was a fraud—who was lost. The very one who incited wrong.

In rage and disappointment, I sunk into delusion and bitterness.

Bitter because my boys' fees were not paid.
Bitter because my best friend did not keep the promise she made, and I never forgave.

I was angry because I stopped having faith. My hate had cast Truelove away.

In lack of understanding, we struggled to build bricks on a sinking ship—steered by a shifty Chief.

What we didn't know was who we were—how did we forget we were the best?

We know better now, it's magnificence in our eyes, and engraved on our hearts.

That which we know has rid us of our suffering.
That which we know, has delivered us from bondage and death.
That which we know, has reconciled old debts.

That we may live as King and Queen—eternal beings, destined to be—in Truelove's holy matrimony.

It was in death I saw—that only true love conquers all.

Offspring

Just when we thought ours was a thing that was lost, Trust empowered us.

Lost in wanderlust, I found my faith—and in new realization, made great haste.

Powerful, I flew from seclusion—to a land I once knew—where Truelove had finally found her bloom.

Dear Lemon,

You died today.

I don't miss you—I don't grieve you.
Love was the tool used to break you.

I'm glad I broke too.

Love,
King

My love, I thought was Lemon was truly Gold—all along, my Mrs. Rose. Doubt had cloaked my eyes, and bitterness had clouded my mind. Hers was that soft ease—strengthened by a thousand seas. She was that kind Spirit, "Edel"—eager to be—'Truelove,' bursting from within.

I had finally woken up from my dream: up—from the ashes of fiery revelry.

I rose King—in me, 'Abba Father's' Spirit: Edel—Golden comforter; His son: Love; and His Majesty: "'Power', 'Sound-mind' and 'Truelove'," whom I humbly refer to as Lion.

At last, I remembered the tall golden girl in the tight—beautifully sewn black dress. Who was never bitter, who was all so sweet; who was Truelove, and quite the treat:

"My Lady Rose"; my Nile, and Gold;
She had always been there, I just didn't know—waiting for me, eager to grow.

Astounded, I was in awe. I could not believe who she was. She said hello—I knew for sure: "my darling Edel"—my love, pure joy.

Edel

Born again, we welcomed each other to new names—and assured one another we will never go away. She smiled and held my arms—as if I were her charm.

We spent the night in warm embrace; we laughed, we cried, we ate and happily danced the night away.

We gathered our families—and cheerfully told our stories! They emphatically forgave, and together, we cut our cake. The arrogance of intuition was surely misplaced.

Our home was full of laughter, and unrivaled banter: Everyone came to share in Truelove's character.

We all thanked God for the end of winter, and said a prayer for spring.

Our house was now a home; full of cheer and full of rose: vibrant sounds of forgotten winters and delightful springs, summer charms and blithe autumn winds.

An eternal spirit dwelled within; a playful spirit—quite the scene: A Love of loves and comforting words—demise was gone, new life was born.

The walls coughed into life; they
had been bitten by sour bite. Once
filled with ashes from regret, they
now stood steady on our chests.
Joy was something that was
seen— not a fathom or a dream.

This day I prayed I would always
know—for sorrow was gone and
Truelove had found a home.

We toasted to delight, and roared
to wondrous sites.

These days, now bright and have
no end. What blinding joy and
sweet rejoice.

Thank God

"What great site to see—Chief Taincy and Carrot hanging merrily from 'Truelove's Tree'."

I married Lion in the warmth of an Apple Summer,
We suffered in the chill of a Lemon Winter,

And loved in the nobility of spring.

We survived the fire of venomous regret

We burned in its passion until rebirth

From its ashes, Edel rose

and

I am. Love

Today, I am proud father of two beautiful boys—two magical boys and God's Lambs, Edel and Love. I am Uncle to six bright nieces, and a daring prince. I am father and Love to my sisters—Truelove tested; Truelove tried; Truelove that will never fail, and will never die.

Today, I am husband to Gold, her name will never grow old— Queen Edel, "Love's Rose": Queen of Queens, and a heart of gold; Queen of Cities and turquoise Princes; Queen of King—Hailed as fair, fair and gold:

> You will live long, Golden Queen:
> You will rule wisely and fairly—
> The people will rise to adore you;
> They have acknowledged you as good.

Truelove brought me out of the darkness, and into God's light.

Today my light shines bright: many have seen, and acknowledge my Father is King—who is Love, Truelove indeed.

Today, I am Love, and I love a Lion.
Today, I am Love and a rather dapper Lion.

Love

I finally figured it out:

Love does not walk out when it does not work out. Love takes its time to help her figure her out—to set her free.

Love is patient and a Queen. Love is. She does not insist on her own way, or my way—She doesn't mind. Love is the only thing that is perfect—the only gift that lasts.

Love is a Lady and a King; Love is a Lion and a Lamb;
Love is simply you, and I.

Lion

My Queen.
Her story begins.

For Lion

Whose love brought me out of the darkness, and into God's light:
I shall write many more for you

Thank You Abba Father, for this Lesson of Love.

Apology letter to Momo

Who will not forgive me for not sharing
when my heart was weary:

> Momo, a man
> must protect his
> wife—for better
> or worse. And a
> wife must honor
> her husband—
> no matter what:

Dear Momo,

I find letters that start with "Sorry" or "I" rather dull. So, let's start this again:

Dear Momo,

My Momo...
Ours is a story I'm saving for last; the truest tale I'd ever write.

I mellowed in your league. It was in your company I found aptitude for poetry: the music lit a dark room; our banter lit its space to suit my Victorian tastes.

Yours was a love I knew I wouldn't forget from the start. Yours is the purest part of my revived heart.

Whilst treating it gently—kindly, I've smothered it. In doing so, I have curbed its growth.

I'm sorry Love. I'm sorry I've starved our friendship of reciprocation. I've been your rock when you let me—is it not fair that I let you be mine?

I see now—how unfair obscurity is in a friendship. I've adjusted.

Will you forgive me?

Love,
King

Guided by the Characteristics of Love
& The Mystery of Resurrection:

The first of the Corinthians, 13 &15:

You are Lion; you are "Truelove"

Developed to the Sound of Elegance

Silence

Thank you

My Father
Lion

My Mother
Beauty

My Siblings
Thank you for the privilege of loving you

My Children
I'll see you soon

Declarations

Chief Taincy
Chief Taincy is well, and at peace
All his children honor him

Carrot
Carrot is a dear friend and successful proprietress.
All the Apples know her name

Edel
Edel is a successful Entrepreneur and the wealthiest woman in Matakar.
She is Mother to many Charities and Executive at The Apple Foundation:
Where we help make good dreams come true

Cocopine
Cocopine is a celebrated International footballer
He is also an affluent Businessman

Beans
Beans is a popular Innovator and Economic Leader
He is changing the world impact-fully

"Today, we live in a big house called home."

Edited by Bamboosticks

Published by
The *Bamboosticks Group*

A **Bamboosticks** Production

Family Tree

Children of the kingdom

Papa & Mama's

Tomato *Love*
Love *Love*
Pepper *Love*
Cranberry *Love*
Peach *Love*
Beans *Love*
Strawberry *Love*
Cocopine *Love*
Carrot *Love*

Pride

Pumpkin *Love*
Lion *Love*
Kelta *Love*
Bran *Love*
Savor *Love*
Kiwi *Love*
Strawberry *Love*
Cakes *Love*
Taincy *Love*

Seed

Edel *Love*
Gwen *Love*
Tompre *Love*
Malakai *love*
Salmonella *Love*
Toluwani "King" *Lion*
Taraoluwa "Edel-Rose" *Lion*
Tiwaloluwa "Isabel" *Lion*
Temitope *Love*
Love *Lion*
Beans *Love*
Kabi *Love*
Tutu *Love*
Tiwa *Love*
Tunu *Love*
Tope *Love*
Tela *Love*
Ife *Love*

All the Fruits

Love's Garden

Carrot Anna Tara Oshoname Tosin Titi Tobi Timi Deola
Mark John Mohammed Love Ireolu Abdulaziz Abba Paul Emmanuel zainab
Arab Rain King Batya Temmy Keisha Anna Shola Mustapha Ike Kingsley Arinze
Ese Baby April Marco-Joseph Ibrahim Zara Eshovo Abu Wafor Blessing Confidence
Abubakar Aramide Valerie Dasha Brynath Dare Femi Kemi Mary Afor Abdulrazaq
Julie Stephen Eguolo Beatrix Bukki Yetunde Emmanuel Rin-Rin Maryam Zunu
Lukonde Augie Bamboosticks James Ali Bee Olumide Phillips Charles Agutu
Yosola Kuku Ife Peach Chisome Abu Sugarcane Danny Deji Bolaji Lyfe Jennings
Chichima Zara Inumidun Charlotte Mayowa Charlie Simbi Yinka Tolu
Gayathri Muyiwa Deji Kunle Beans Foghor Bee Camil Junior Kelechi Ngozi
Funto Dupe Ugli Fruit Abadom Wild Blueberrie Igbo Red Apple Coconut
Pineapple Custard Apple Abo Chibueze Chinechezirim Yagazie Chinelo
God Ike Wh Chikezie Supreme Victoria Ajala Luck Ganiru Twins Idogbe
Good Ginikachukwu Andreea Olaniyi Hassana Ibekwe Agreement
Hassan Iberedemobong Ifekristi Light Christ Igbo Here Ibironke
Family Happiness Idaramfon Efik Ibibio Ife Mofoluwakemi Blessing
Yoruba Cup Ir Madam Bomi Okpere Long Okwute Olabisi Oladele
Home Oladosu Moon Olajide Yejide Kno Olalekan Olaoluwajuwon
Lion Zaki Hausa Peter Hariya Zoputa Protector Uzodimma Gatee
Ayers Olaseni Easily Boysenberries Olayemi Timi Ifechi Ifede Love
Alive Hauwa Zauna Flowe Aduke Ifeoluwapo Ifetundun Love Sweet
Tree Igitioluwotilaiye Root Journey Ijeoma LifBeef Ikechukwu
Power Ikeoluwa Clementine Ikponmwosa Kparobo Leader Obi
Heart Igbo Emeka Obianauju Peace Zikorachukwud Paul Lewis
Abu Zoputan Ileara Child Ilozumba Imbiana Unity Inegbedion
Oba King Good Character Nsedu Tiwa Kingship Kristibueze
Machie Sleepp Iretomiwa Blessing Kaodinakachi Destiny Leaf
Mojisola Fortune Obioma Gem Modupeore k MongoFamous
Nwamaka Patience Ndidi Maka Advantage Goodwill Nkwo
Market Creator Nwaoma Oban Obiefune Monjolaoluwa Hausa
Nagodeallah Nkeoma Good Beauty Robert Chinwe Uwailomwan
Oluchi Chetachukwu Yetunde Olusola Utibe Marvelous Okonkwo
Ify Pi Solomon Chinyere ChiOlufemiOlugbala Olukayode
Joy Olumoroti Stand Olusegun Victory Yoruba Chinmakodim
Udumelue Crown Honor Pride Olonunyomi Olisa God Igbo
Okechuku Destiny Isoken Conten Itunu Iwenjiora Iyabo Iyawa
Hausa Jaiyesimi Jesutise Jesus Jideofor Respect Juba Awakes
Izukanne Light Ihekristi Christ Igbo Valerie Carrisa Olatundun
Sweet King Abaeze Watermelon Olive King Branch Igbo Guava
Sharon Plum Orange Chimaobi Heart Sugarcane Abayomi
Water Coconut Abi Abu Yusuf Joy Yoruba Adaoma Lady Yabani
Guy Pierce Abayomnunkoje God Life Quince Raisins Durains
Feijoa Guava Clementine Maradol Sour Hap Cactus Pear Saraki
Barbados Cantaloupe Blood Orange Brown Turkey Fig Yemi Kemi
Femi Monday Sanitubi Yusuf Papaya Strawberry Abebi Hauwa Wale
Prince Itunu Iyabo Page JJa Abegunde Jesus Abeni Abdurazaq
Omotola Iya-beji Bowale Sugarcane Chiemeka ChimezieSugar Apple
Naruto Abeo Cactus Peace Tubosun Zainab Adewale Prince Anthony
ChidubemGuave Abidemi Dew Mango Otumba Kuku Sanit Abubakar
Seun Tola Lola Prince ChilotumKiki Sasuke Abidugun War Rain
Bankai Omotoriola Lola Adeniyi Tope Omotoso Oluwa UdAbiodun
Naima Zakari Festival Love Peace Debra-Louise Adebambo Crown Me
ChimbuchimKuku Abiodun Nike Ayelowo Brazil Abidemi Chigoziem
Abdulahi Chikanma Efik Ibibio AbOlumide Abioye Eleanor-Rose Adaora
Daughter Igbo Isamotu Olalekan Destitute KokumorAbioye Ibrahim Abolanle
Mohammed Straberry-Papaya Abomeli Achebe Goddess Precious Love Gold
Edel-Rose Hanuna Achike Steady Winner Igbo Rami Achutebe Adebamgbe
Dwells LyfeAda-afo Third Solabomi Yetunde Precious Yewande Paul Sukanmi
Olabisi Oyenikan Jospeh Adewale Rukewwe Coco rIN-rIN Adamma Daughter
Beauty IgboAdankwo Oshoname Kiwi XiiStrawberry-Guava Adebisi Momo Adebiyi
Batya Adebowale Marian Adeboye Title Ajaka TopSegun Adedayo Tayo Adedeji
Two Iyabo Adedoyin Sweet Tosin Adefolake Tobi Adejola AnnaSola Adekola Jolomi
Adeleke Happiness Daniella Adeleye Honorable Onome Adenike Kate Cherish Hauwa
Adenike Femi Adeola Mojo Adeolu Fig Knowledge Adetosoye Sopuruchi Ike ApeSonubi
Aderinola Ire Aderiyike Pam Crown Yoruba Maroon Adesehinwa Shounubi Adesewa
Emmanuel Adesola Goke Adesola Robert Adetokunbo Colver Ki Adetokunbo Tarzan Tayo
Oyo-VApple Suleiman Adetowumi Zakari Well Kite Adewemimo Bayo-Adewole Royalty Akamere
MomoAdeyemI Adeyemo Crown Befits Child Righteous Adigun Adimabua Destiniy Aigbokai Tenm

"And this garden shall bear good fruit".
AMEN

A Cub's Commission;

Truelove's vision

"Truelove's creed"
"To help make good dreams come true"

"All that we do is committed to the service of Love, and
each other; what in itself is Marriage and God"

"The Lord's Prayer; **Our Prayer"**

PURPOSE   To serve God—in Spirit, Truth & Understanding: Executing His
will on earth—as it is in Heaven— through divine wisdom,
knowledge, strength and wealth."

DIRECTION   Learn what/how it is in heaven
> *What is Heaven's infrastructure?*
> *What is heavenly food—how does it taste?*
> *What is Heavens standard for Living, Teaching,
> Learning, Loving?*

Provide great food; "Heavens daily bread"
Provide great infrastructure and associated governance to
the Earth
Teach divine living, value & Productivity to Love's kin
Praise, worship and thank God, ceaselessly

INTERESTS   Infrastructure/ Productivity: "Platform to build good life"
Lifestyle: "A set of divine attitudes, habits, and possessions to
secure an ease and attainment of good life"
Food: "Nutritious substance eaten in order to maintain good
life and grow"
Education: "An enlightening experience that prepares you
for the most enjoyable way to live a good life"

EDUCATION   "The Book of Life"

VALUES   True Love
Culture of commission   Integrity

Service

Loyalty

Excellence

Adaptability & Innovation

Value Addition

The Love and Lion Series:

Love and a Lion

Edel
Love
Lion
Edel and King
Love and a Beast
A Lady and her King

Lionheart

The best way to honor a man, is to learn the things he loves and love them completely:

I love God.

The best way to love a woman is to accept her entirely:

I love Lion.

About the Author

Toluwani King is a philanthropist and infrastructure strategist.

Printed in the United States
By Bookmasters